Lush
Life

Lush Life

Food & Drinks from the Garden

Valerie Rice

FOREWORD BY SUZANNE GOIN

WINE COMMENTARY BY RAJ PARR

PHOTOGRAPHY BY GEMMA & ANDREW INGALLS

PROSPECT
·PARK·
BOOKS

FOR MY HUSBAND, AJ, AND DAUGHTERS, AVA & LILY.
Thank you for your love, encouragement, patience, and
sense of humor, every day, and certainly throughout this
entire book process. I love you more.

& FOR MY PARENTS, NICOLE AND GENE RONALD,
who taught me to try something new every day,
and to always dream big.

Contents

Embracing Every Moment in the Kitchen & Garden

BY SUZANNE GOIN

I have been lucky enough to enjoy more than a few meals (and drinks and bottles of wine!) at Valerie Rice's stunning Southern California paradise of a home, and I have to say that whoever came up with the title *Lush Life* has hit the nail directly on the head. But it's not just the beautiful setting, the glorious garden, or the flavorful and captivating food and drink—the lushness stems right from Valerie's heart and soul. Her passion for gardening, cooking, and entertaining is a triumvirate of riches to be enjoyed by anyone who finds themselves fortunate enough to be welcomed into her home. This passion and love for ingredients, where they come from, and the art of time around the table are Valerie's magic, and she has captured that spirit and meticulously passed it along in these pages.

In her seemingly effortless, casual way, Valerie brings us into her world, which always begins in the garden. When you start with beautiful produce straight from your garden or local farmers market, you are halfway there, and you'll find yourself in a spot that is already far ahead of your average cook. Local ingredients in the peak of the season pop with color and vitality. Not needing too much manipulation, hyper-seasonal ingredients instead benefit from a gentle, caring hand that exercises restraint, coaxing the best from them and honoring each vegetable's innate deliciousness. The garden will tell you which ingredients work well together—the old adage "what grows together goes together" steers you toward such meant-to-be combinations as Valerie's Golden Beets & Blood Oranges with Citrus Vinaigrette; Blistered Asparagus with Pistachios, Green Garlic & Chives; and Tomato & Stone Fruit Salad with Sesame Maple Dressing.

Jacques Pépin once told me that if you give ten cooks a chicken to roast, the end result will be ten very different roast chickens. This is where the cook's personality and specific affinities come into play. The recipes in this book very clearly highlight Valerie's style and are so very particularly "her." Living in Santa Barbara means acknowledging its deep-rooted and authentic Mexican influence—Valerie's famous tamales are to die for, and her Halibut Ceviche will put you right on the beach. Informed by her passion for travel and her lust for life, Valerie infuses the surprising indulgence of a bit of richness into her vegetable-focused cooking. Risottos are creamy; spaghetti carbonara is spiked with Champagne; chicken is roasted in terracotta; and Moroccan spices, lime, honey, tahini, chimichurri, and shishito peppers appear throughout the recipes, bringing hints of spice, acid, and richness to her lush garden cuisine. This balance of garden ingredients, unexpected flavors and pairings, and craveable combinations is the great charm of Valerie's bold cooking.

And don't forget the cocktails and the desserts! As beautiful and satisfying as every meal is at Casa Rice, the experience begins right when you walk in the door—the garden comes to you first in the guise of a perfectly balanced and refreshing Spring Loquat Shrub Cocktail, or a Strawberry Mezcal Margarita in the heat of summer, or, in the fall, an ethereal Lemon Rose Martini. Part of living a lush life is embracing every moment, and that is exactly what Valerie does in life and in this book. She takes every possible occasion to weave her garden into the experience and to welcome the reader, as her guest, into her world. Desserts are no exception. From the elegant Red Rhubarb Amaretto Torte, to the adorable Lemon Chiffon Cupcakes with Rose Petals, to the classic Pink Lady Apple Tarte Tatin, Valerie's desserts perfectly walk the line of truly honoring seasonal ingredients while still being decadent and undeniably irresistible.

I think I have been waiting for this book for almost as long as it has been in Valerie's head. When an expert has such a deep and true passion, it's a joy to get into her mind and understand how the creative process works. In this book, Valerie spells it all out. We see how at the same moment that she is taking direction from her spring garden to guide her menus, she is planning the planting of her summer garden as well. She shares her gardening tips, teaching us to always be looking forward to the next season. I love the Pantry Recipes & Gifts from the Garden section as well. For anyone with a garden or anyone who works as closely with farmers as I do, you know you'll have those moments when you will never be able to use up all those persimmons or tomatoes. Valerie's solutions—like her Dried Persimmon Slices and Cherry Tomato & Gin Jam and her Apricot Jam with Lemon Verbena, not to mention her tips for drying herbs and chilies—are beyond useful and delightful. I hope you will throw yourself into Valerie's lush, garden-focused world and feel the joy that comes from cooking directly from the source to nurture and feed the people you love. For me, as for Valerie, there is no greater pleasure in this not-always-so-lush life!

SUZANNE GOIN is a James Beard Award–winning chef and restaurateur and the author of *Sunday Suppers at Lucques* and *The A.O.C. Cookbook*.

It's All About the Season

YOU DON'T HAVE TO COOK FANCY OR COMPLICATED MASTERPIECES
—JUST GOOD FOOD FROM FRESH INGREDIENTS.
— JULIA CHILD

A foundational concept behind this book—and my life—is to eat foods that are sourced as close to home as possible and synchronized with the seasons. The longer that produce has existed off the vine, and the farther its journey to reach your kitchen, the fewer nutrients (and more preservatives) it will have—and the more tasteless it will be. Big Farm-a has become artful at creating long-lasting produce that looks like it was plucked from a cornucopia painting by Giuseppe Arcimboldo. But too often that luscious-looking tomato tastes like corked packing peanuts drowned in ketchup.

I may be late to parties and doctor's appointments, but I'm always on time for what's in season. I've learned that when you eat and drink with the seasons, your food tastes better and looks gorgeous. It's also more varied, because while the techniques are the same, the ingredients are ever changing. Plus, eating seasonally takes the guesswork out of knowing what to cook—just go with what's freshest. The great news is that today there are more opportunities than ever to be a seasonal locavore: home and community gardens, farmers markets, online ordering, and even, with luck, your corner grocery.

Until I began writing this book, I didn't realize how much my parents' heritage influenced my cooking. My mom is Belgian, and my father's family is from Calabria, Italy; many of my favorite recipes meld their marriage onto a plate. When I was a child, we sometimes visited family in Belgium in the summer. My grandmother, Make (which means "little mother" in Flemish), had the most spectacular vegetable garden—I felt like I was walking through the pages of *The Secret Garden*. For a kid who grew up in a planned community behind California's Orange Curtain, this was culture shock. I decided at a pretty young age that wherever I ended up, I wanted to grow veggies just like my Make.

My dream came true when we bought our first home in Santa Barbara. Somebody pinch me: the Pacific Ocean in our backyard, the Mediterranean weather, the year-round gardening, the interesting people... *and* we get to eat Mexican food all the time. Southern California's Mexican culture has inspired so many meals from my kitchen garden. Side by side, I have learned some essential

Mexican cooking techniques from a few wonderful Latinas I have worked with over the years. I am grateful for where I live, and for what these women have taught me, every single day.

When I cook, I look to my garden for inspiration. Becoming a gardener has taught me so much, including patience and planning, two things that don't come naturally. I planted my first garden eighteen years ago because back then, I couldn't find certain ingredients I'd fallen in love with while traveling, like romanesco and mâche in the fall and winter and fresno peppers and San Marzano tomatoes in the summer. My obsession with those foods made me decide to grow them myself. Starting a garden led to composting, and next thing you know, I was raising chickens for eggs (and companionship—those chickens are so darn sweet) and bees for pollination and honey. My backyard gradually became both an oasis and a study in trial and error. After a few years, I decided to become a Master Gardener through the University of California Extension program. That's not necessary, however, to maintain a good, simple kitchen garden, and in this book I pass along some tips on how to get started on a garden of your own (see page 279).

My husband has spent the better part of his adult life collecting and learning about wine. When we met, our romance was a pairing made in culinary heaven—he brought the wine, and I made the food (even if it was in a shoe-box-size kitchen). Cooking with wine in mind made me ultra-conscientious about not overpowering or over "ingredient-ing" the food, allowing the beautiful wine to shine.

As I cooked, I learned through making mistakes in the kitchen, eating a lot, and reading books to source and edit ingredients. Travel also helped me learn. My husband and I took advantage of our ability to work remotely to travel. We are not skiers or surfers; we are eaters and drinkers. So our destinations have typically revolved around food. Italy, Japan, Spain, France, Mexico, Austria, Hong Kong—all have influenced my cooking. I have a memory for food and can tell you, years later, the exact meal we ate on a particular day, but I couldn't possibly remember the name of the darn hotel where we stayed. As I write this, COVID-19 has grounded all travel, and the world is an anxious place. When a pang of sadness sets in, we pop open a bottle of rosé, and I pick some Swiss chard from the garden and make a quiche. Voilà—we are in Provence. We are lucky to have inspiration from trips past and to have so many ingredients at our fingertips.

THE RECIPES

I'm an equal-opportunity eater. I always joke that I wish I had some food allergies or restrictions, because I do eat everything. Most of all, however, I am a home cook who relishes the opportunity to cook for people I love. Nothing delights me more than a table full of happy, well-fed guests. My goal as a home cook is to cook the cleanest, most flavorful food, tied to the rhythms of the earth and the seasons, in the simplest way and with the least amount of dishes. Words to live by, right? Scientists call this practice "chronobiology." I call it nutritious and frickin' delicious.

The recipes in these pages are the ones I make on repeat, whether it be for a school-night family dinner or a dinner party for twelve. My favorite part? While they taste and look fantastic, they aren't fussy or meltdown-inducing. Seasonal, fresh food just needs to be simply prepared—let the ingredients do most of the work for you. That being said, I am perhaps a little obsessive about sourcing great ingredients. I buy organic whenever possible, and I seek out grass-fed beef, free-range and air-chilled poultry, wild-caught fish, and full-fat, grass-fed dairy—basically the same foods my grandparents ate in Belgium. Being a lover of the land and a gardening nut, I am committed to organic gardening practices, and I grow heirloom plants from seeds without genetic modification. Speaking of ingredients, I'm particular about salt. I call for Diamond Crystal kosher, because it has no additives and its granules are larger, which make it less salty than other salts. And I finish dishes with a flaky sea salt like Jacobsen's—it adds a wonderful pop of seasoning after a dish is plated.

I've presented the recipes by season, beginning with spring, when the garden really likes to show off. Each season's section starts with the lowdown on that season's star ingredients, as well as tips on what to plant for the next season—I'm hoping to inspire even non-gardeners to plant one of those ingredients in a pot outside the door. Next, you'll find cocktails and appetizers to whet your whistle, followed by mains, sides, and sweets. Before I get to those seasonal chapters, I start out with advice on staples, spices, herbs, and kitchen tools. After the seasonal chapters, I share my favorite pantry recipes and gifts from the garden, as well as some advice for starting a garden and setting up a bar. All of the recipes within the seasons can be mixed and matched, and there are lots of do-aheads. The more you make in advance, the less you'll be sweating through your charmeuse when the doorbell rings.

THE DRINKS

Just about every cocktail recipe was inspired by flavors from our travels—margaritas in Mexico City, martinis in London, negronis in Florence, amaretto sours in Tokyo (yes, that was a thing and it was delightful)—sometimes given a twist with what grows in my yard. Each drink is made with just a few ingredients. The recipes yield at least two servings, because even if you're drinking alone, you might as well have one for each hand. In general, I save cocktails for more special occasions (although don't ask me about my habits during the COVID quarantine), and I don't normally drink them with meals—I might savor one on occasion as I cook dinner or sip one while sharing appetizers with friends.

We typically drink wine with dinner. Harsh as it may sound, I do not set a seat for over-oaked, overworked, mass-produced wine at my table. I spend a lot of time tending my garden and sourcing quality ingredients, so my husband and I try to do the same with wine. We are constantly seeking out small-production wines made in the traditional style of their region. Wine is meant to complement the food, not overwhelm it, so we look for balanced offerings that marry well with the meal. One suggestion to consider more often is Champagne. Typically it is reserved only for holidays and very special occasions, but it's a delight with many meals, and nowadays there are many wonderful small, artisanal producers, some of whom make surprisingly affordable Champagnes. So go ahead—pop a bottle to enjoy with a weeknight meal.

RAJ TELLS ME

Because my husband is a wine enthusiast, we have a lot of dear friends in the world of wine. One of them is globally known sommelier turned winemaker Rajat Parr, a good friend of nearly two decades. Although he would not want me to say this, Raj is one of the most influential wine experts of our generation, with three James Beard awards to his name. He is fantastically talented, thoughtful, and kindhearted, and he was generous enough with his time and expertise to help me with this book. We sat down together and went through all of the entrées, as well as some desserts and appetizers, to make wine-pairing suggestions. You'll spot these with the lead **RAJ TELLS ME...** after many recipes. You can ask your local wine shop to help find the bottles, or enter the name at wine-searcher.com to find them online (you're welcome).

This book has been a longtime dream of mine, and my hope is that, if I've done this right, it will become your trusted guide, splattered and wine-stained with notes alongside the recipes that you build into your repertoire. My greatest honor would be if you cook the hell out of this book, hopefully with at least a few home-grown ingredients, and have a fantastic time in the process. Here we go.

Spring

Spring:
The Double-Joy Season

I LOVE SPRING ANYWHERE, BUT IF I COULD CHOOSE
I WOULD ALWAYS GREET IT IN A GARDEN.
— RUTH STOUT

Spring brings double joy to my garden: first, harvesting the new bounty of spring treasures, and second, digging in the dirt to start planting for the flavors of summer. After the somewhat sparse harvest baskets of winter, suddenly I'm faced with an overflow of lush, gorgeous produce: fava beans, sugar snap and sweet peas, breakfast radishes, brassicas, new potatoes, loads of lettuces, loquats, alpine strawberries, rhubarb, and citrus of all sorts fill our veggie beds and baskets. Everything, and I mean everything, is blossoming—from the roses first off the hook bloom to the pineapple guava trees—the thought of which makes me sneeze and smile all at the same time. In spring, preparing delicious meals just becomes a matter of how to best show off these natural goodies, and there are so many simple ways to incorporate all of the sweetness of this season.

It wasn't until I started raising chickens that I realized there is definitely a season for eggs, too. It's no wonder eggs are a center-stage star for Easter, because there certainly is a ramp-up in egg production in the springtime.

Spring is when the mid-winter entertaining lull lifts and impromptu outdoor cocktail hours and garden dinner parties kick into gear again. I often anchor my outdoor table with pretty potted plants. It's an easy way to make sure things look inviting, and there's no need to fuss with cut flowers for the table. If the flowers in the garden are in bloom, it's easy to create a few small bouquets to tuck in among the green.

This is the season that always fills me with Zyrtec and the thrill of possibility, inspired by the new and longer light, and the blooms, buds, and bounty of the garden. The recipes in this section include many of my absolute favorites. From garden to kitchen and back outside again, where a fresh, simple dinner surrounded by the scent of fresh soil mingles with the sweetness of those first roses, spring seduces again and again.

WHAT TO PLANT NOW

If you grow these items, you'll be able to cook from your garden in the next chapter. I mark my calendar at the spring equinox to get planting for summer. For planting tips see page 279.

CUCUMBERS: PERSIAN & LEMON CUCUMBER	HERBS: LEMON VERBENA, THAI SWEET BASIL, GENOVESE BASIL, CILANTRO	SQUASH: GREY, RONDE DE NICE, COSTATA ROMANESCO
HEIRLOOM EGGPLANT: LISTADA DE GANDIA, ROSA BIANCA, EDIRNE PURPLE STRIPED, AND ROSITA	WILD PURPLE TOMATILLO	PEPPERS: FRESNO, SHISHITO, PADRÓN, CHILE DE ARBOL
TOMATOES: SUNGOLD, YELLOW BRANDYWINE, SAN MARZANO, BLACK KRIM, MUSHROOM BASKET (DETERMINANT)	BEANS: HARICOTS VERTS AND DRAGON TONGUE BUSH BEANS	ALPINE STRAWBERRIES

Spring Recipes

Spring Drinks

1.

2.

3.

4

5.

6.

Gin Salty Dog with Fresh Mint

MAKES 2 COCKTAILS

Bright, sweet, and bold (no, I'm not talking about myself)—Ruby Red grapefruits are lip-smackingly delicious. No need to add any sweetener to this type of God-made perfection. In California, grapefruit season generally lasts from January through August. If you can't find Ruby Red, try other varieties like Oro Blanco, Pink, or Star Ruby. Whatever you do, don't use pasteurized store-bought juice. The flavor is not even close to being as delicious. The longer the grapefruit sits in a bowl on your counter, the sweeter it will become. Sometimes if the flavor is too sweet, I'll add a squeeze of lime. I love the freshness of the mint in this cocktail—it draws on all of the delectable botanical notes found in gin.

If you're an anti-gin person (I know, I know, you had a bad gin experience in college), you can substitute vodka. But gin is more traditional. Give it a go—you might be a convert.

2 tablespoons flaky sea salt
10 ounces (1¼ cups) fresh grapefruit juice
   (from 1 to 2 grapefruits)
4 ounces (½ cup) gin, such as Ford's, or Old Raj
2 thin grapefruit wedges and 2 fresh mint sprigs
   (garnish)

Pour sea salt onto a small saucer. Dip the rim of a double old-fashioned glass in the juice, then dip it in salt (if you want to be fancy, just dip half of the glass in the salt). Fill glasses with ice. Stir the juice and gin in a small pitcher (or mixing glass) and pour into salt-rimmed glasses. Garnish with grapefruit and mint.

Campari & Tangerine

MAKES 2 COCKTAILS

While this combo is most commonly known as a brunch drink, it's also a light and lovely evening option for those who are partial to a negroni but not so fond of all the booze.

In Ojai, Pixie tangerines become available in March. They are packed with flavor and that perfect mix of sweetness and acidity. You can also make this cocktail with Satsumas (late fall) or Kishu tangerines in the winter.

6 Satsuma tangerines, peeled
4 ounces (½ cup) Campari
Angostura bitters
Fresh mint sprigs and tangerine wedges (garnish)

Purée tangerines in a pitcher using an immersion blender (or purée in a regular blender). Fill a small pitcher (or mixing glass) ¾ full with ice; add 1 cup of the purée, Campari, and a dash of bitters. Stir to chill. Fill 2 rocks glasses with ice. Strain cocktail into glasses. Garnish with mint and tangerine.

KITCHEN NOTE: I learned to juice whole peeled fruit via an immersion blender at a fantastic six-seat bar in Tokyo (see Kitchen Tools, page 278), and it inspired me to try this method at home. Now I won't do it any other way. Ever.

Blood Orange Margaritas

MAKES 2 COCKTAILS

Tart, delicious, and so beautiful, blood orange season is something to celebrate. Supermarkets often stock blood oranges that have been shipped in from a land far, far away, and I find that they can smell dank and are soft to the touch. It's best to purchase them at the farmers market. Or, better yet, if you live in a warm climate like we have in Santa Barbara (where the days are warm and the nights are cool), buy a tree and plant it in your yard. If you're tight on space, grow a dwarfed variety in a large pot. You'll know the citrus is ready to be picked when the peel looks slightly red like it was dusted in rust.

4 ounces (½ cup) tequila
2 ounces (¼ cup) fresh blood orange juice (from 1 orange)
1½ ounces (3 tablespoons) Cointreau
1 ounce (2 tablespoons) fresh lime juice (from 1 to 2 limes)
1 lime wedge
Flaky sea salt
2 blood orange wheels (garnish)

Mix tequila, blood orange juice, Cointreau, and lime juice in a small pitcher or glass measuring cup. *(Margarita mix can be made ahead. Cover and refrigerate up to 2 hours.)*

Run a lime wedge around the lip of 2 short glasses to moisten, then dip into a saucer filled with sea salt. Fill glasses with ice. Add blood orange wheels to glasses and fill with margarita mix.

Three-Ingredient Mai Tai

MAKES 2 COCKTAILS

The mai tai is one of my mom's favorite cocktails. I think with every sip she gets transported back to wearing a cotton bikini on the warm beaches of Hawaii in the '70s. I never used to make them at home because the ingredient list was lofty. With some simple editing, however, we pared things back a little, and the result was delicious, Don Ho worthy, and simple.

In the spring, I garnish the drink with the flowers from my pineapple guava tree—it's SO pretty, and the flowers taste almost like a lychee. In the summer, I load the cocktail with juicy pineapple spears and lots of fresh mint from the garden.

4 ounces (½ cup) dark rum, such as Gosling's or Lemon Hart
2 ounces (¼ cup) fresh lime juice (from 3 limes)
1 ounce (2 tablespoons) orgeat syrup
Pineapple wedges (garnish)
Orange or lime wheels (garnish)

Fill cocktail shaker ¾ full with ice; add rum, lime juice, and syrup, and shake like the dickens—I count to eight. Strain into 2 coupe glasses. Garnish with pineapple and orange.

BAR NOTE: Orgeat is an almond and orange flower syrup and is super handy to have in your bar. It's a delicious nonalcoholic sweetener excellent in coffee or other beverages. You can make homemade versions, or try Liquid Alchemist or Fee Brothers.

Citrus Blossom Pisco Sour

MAKES 2 COCKTAILS

If you live in California, you probably know the amazing scent of citrus trees blooming in the springtime. This simple syrup takes on those wonderfully fragrant notes and makes them palatable. My chef friend Erika Petote introduced me to Pisco, a type of brandy, and it's strong—like more than 80 proof! One is fun, two is wild, three is messy... Don't say I didn't warn you.

If you don't have citrus blossoms, you can mix store-bought orange flower water (which you can find at most Middle Eastern markets) into the cold syrup. Start by adding ⅛ teaspoon, then taste before adding more.

ORANGE BLOSSOM SIMPLE SYRUP
20 fresh orange blossoms or mixture of citrus
    blossoms
10 citrus leaves
1½ cups water
1 cup sugar

COCKTAIL
2 ounces (¼ cup) Orange Blossom Simple Syrup
6 ounces (¾ cup) Pisco (see Bar Tips & Tools, page 283)
2 ounces (¼ cup) fresh lime juice (from 3 limes)
½ ounce (1 tablespoon) egg white
Angostura bitters
Fresh orange blossoms (garnish)

FOR SYRUP: Gently wash blossoms and leaves in a bowl full of cool water—this helps displace any bugs or small particles of dirt. In a heavy large saucepan, bring 1½ cups water to a boil. Add the citrus blossoms and leaves, reduce heat, and simmer for 10 minutes, stirring occasionally. Strain blossom liquid into a large measuring cup; discard solids. Mix sugar into the hot blossom liquid and stir to dissolve. Cool syrup. Makes about 1 cup. *(Syrup can be made 1 week ahead. Cover and refrigerate.)*

FOR COCKTAIL: Fill a large cocktail shaker ¾ full with ice. Add ¼ cup Orange Blossom Simple Syrup, Pisco, lime juice, and egg white, and shake like the dickens. Strain contents into 2 rocks glasses. Add 2 drops of bitters on top of the foam. Garnish with orange blossoms.

To make a big batch for a crowd, mix 3 cups Pisco, 1 cup lime juice, 1 cup syrup, 4 egg whites, and 24 to 32 ice cubes in a pitcher. Pulse ingredients using an immersion blender (or transfer mixture to a regular blender and pulse to blend).

GARDEN NOTE: In the late winter and early spring, citrus trees in our yard are teeming with blossoms. Lots of blossoms don't necessarily translate to a high fruit yield, so I utilize the abundance of blossoms in cocktails. You can make this recipe with virtually any type of unsprayed citrus—limes, grapefruit, lemons, oranges—all with great success. Pick the blossoms and leaves in the morning, before the sun has hit the buds, and select the smallest, most tender leaves. This concoction of blossoms and leaves makes a beautiful tea, which we enjoy often as our citrus trees bloom. The addition of the sugar makes the simple syrup.

Loquat Shrub Cocktail

MAKES UP TO 10 COCKTAILS

The loquat tree is one of those iconic backyard beauties that so many people have in Santa Barbara, but no one knows what in the heck to do with the high yield of fruit each spring. The small tropical-tasting fruit (like a peach that had a baby with a mango) is delicious but is riddled with seeds and often needs to be peeled for recipes. This shrub cocktail is the easiest and most successful way to deal with the massive collection of fruit. No peeling; just cut in half and pop the seeds out.

A shrub is a vinegar- and syrup-based drink that both quenches your thirst and wets your whistle. Normally, a shrub is served with bourbon or rum, and both are great options, but you can really pick your favorite liquor. This drink could also be made with no liquor (it could happen…).

LOQUAT SHRUB
6 cups chopped, seeded, ripe loquats (about 3 pounds)
¾ cup sugar
½ cup raw apple cider vinegar
¼ cup unseasoned rice vinegar

COCKTAIL
Loquat Shrub
Bourbon, gin, or tequila (optional)
Chilled sparkling water
Sliced fresh loquats and mint sprigs (garnish)

FOR SHRUB: Mix all ingredients in a pot and bring to a boil. Continue to boil for 3 minutes, pressing the loquats with the head of a small whisk or potato masher to crush. Cover the pot, remove from heat, and cool completely. Strain into a large measuring cup; discard solids. Makes about 2 cups. *(Shrub can be made 5 days ahead. Cover and refrigerate.)*

FOR EACH COCKTAIL: Fill a double old-fashioned glass with ice. Add 3 tablespoons of the shrub and ¼ cup bourbon, gin, or tequila, if using. Top with sparkling water. Garnish with loquats and mint.

Golden Negroni with Bourbon, Kumquat & Thyme

MAKES 2 COCKTAILS

This drink is similar to a white negroni with sweet, bitter, and herbal notes, but it's made with bourbon (yes, bourbon—yum!). Search out Suze, a French bitter aperitif made from the gentian root—with its citrusy undertones, it complements the kumquats. We have several kumquat trees in our yard, and this is certainly one of my favorite ways to use these tiny gems. The kumquats give this drink an awesome tang. In this recipe it's served straight up, but it's also delicious over a big cube of ice in a rocks glass.

6 kumquats, sliced

1 fresh thyme sprig

3 ounces (¼ cup plus 2 tablespoons) bourbon

3 ounces (¼ cup plus 2 tablespoons) Lillet Blanc

1 ounce (2 tablespoons) Suze gentian liqueur

Kumquat slices, fresh thyme leaves or blossoms (garnish)

Using the handle of a wooden spoon, smash 6 sliced kumquats and thyme sprig in a cocktail shaker. Fill ¾ full with ice; add bourbon, Lillet Blanc, and Suze. Shake vigorously, counting to eight, and then strain into 2 small cocktail coupes or martini glasses. Garnish with kumquat and thyme.

GARDEN NOTE: | I grow both French and English thyme in pots outside my kitchen door. Either variety will work in this drink; the English has soft, pliable stems, while the French has hardy, woody stems, which make it easier to remove the leaves. The plants are not only drought tolerant, but a lovely addition to the garden. If the thyme in your garden is flowering, pick the pretty light purple blossoms to use as a garnish.

Spring Crudités with Whipped Feta-Piquillo Dip & Mini Pitas

6 SERVINGS

Springtime crudités usually involve a collection of "rabbit food," as my husband calls it, right from the garden. Choose an assortment that is Peter Rabbit worthy—breakfast radishes, market carrots, Japanese turnips, purple cauliflower, and sugar snap peas make for a pretty and yummy combination that truly reflects the season. Crudités are also delicious with Julie's Classic Ranch (page 92), Garden Hummus (page 149), and Herbalicious White Bean Dip (page 212).

My friend Kim Schiffer, a private chef in Santa Barbara and quite possibly the most lovely, compassionate, and flavor-obsessed person in my orbit, shared a version of this dip recipe with me years ago. Cheesy and peppery, it's one of my very favorite dips. We laugh that it is the "Montecito" version of pimento cheese; practically everyone who tries it wants the recipe. Leftovers are great as a spread on a veggie sandwich.

After opening a feta brick (I usually find good ones at Trader Joe's or Middle Eastern markets), place it in a clean glass storage jar and cover with fresh water. By discarding the water it comes in and replacing it with fresh, you can extend the shelf life considerably.

1 6-ounce brick of sheep's milk feta cheese, crumbled (1¼ cups)

3 roasted whole piquillo peppers from a jar, packed in water, drained

¼ cup extra-virgin olive oil

3 tablespoons fresh Meyer lemon juice (from 1 medium lemon)

2 teaspoons grated Meyer lemon zest (from 1 medium lemon)

2 teaspoons dried Aleppo pepper (see Spice Drawer, page 274)

½ teaspoon smoked paprika

¼ teaspoon cayenne pepper

⅛ teaspoon flaky sea salt

Assorted crudités

Mini Pita Bread (recipe follows)

In a food processor, blend feta, peppers, oil, juice, zest, spices, and salt for a good 3 minutes, stopping to scrape down the sides with a rubber spatula. Taste for seasoning, adding more salt or spices depending on your taste buds. Serve with crudités and pita. *(Dip can be made 2 days ahead. Cover and refrigerate in an airtight container. Bring to room temperature before serving.)*

Mini Pita Bread / MAKES 24

After making countless types of flatbread, boules, pitas, and pizzas with multiple different flours and starters, I realized that just about any flatbread dough recipe can be made into a pita. Combine it with whipped feta, crudités, baby artichokes (page 36), and marinated olives (page 210) to make a delicious mezze platter, or tuck in some lamb meatballs and tomato jam (page 269).

This is a very forgiving and flexible dough recipe—you can also use it to make pizza, or brush it with olive oil and grill it to make a flatbread.

2½ cups bread flour

1 teaspoon Diamond Crystal kosher salt

2 teaspoons Nigella seeds or sesame seeds (optional)

7 grams (1 envelope) active dry yeast

¾ cup lukewarm water (105°F to 115°F)

⅓ cup plain Greek yogurt

In a large bowl, whisk flour, salt, and seeds (if using). In a small bowl, mix yeast and water. Once little bubbles start to form on the top of the yeast mixture, about 10 minutes (this means the yeast is good to use and active), mix it into the dry ingredients, then add the yogurt. Stir together with a wooden spoon or your hands until the water is incorporated and dough begins to form. Turn dough out onto the work surface and knead until the dough is smooth and elastic, or about 5 minutes. Place dough in a large, clean bowl; cover with plastic wrap and let stand in a warm spot in your kitchen. The dough needs to double in size, about 1 hour.

Place a baking stone or heavy sheet pan in the middle of your oven and preheat to 425°F. Dust a clean, dry work surface with flour. Punch the dough down to release the air, then turn the dough out onto the work surface. Divide the dough into quarters and then roll each piece into a log. Cut each log into 6 pieces to make a total of 24 balls. Cover the balls with a slightly damp kitchen towel.

Working in batches, add a little dusting of flour to your work surface and, using your hands, flatten each ball into a pancake. Use a rolling pin to roll each into a 4-inch round. Dust the baking stone or sheet pan with flour. Carefully place about 6 pitas at a time on the hot surface. Cook about 10 minutes or until the pitas puff up and are golden brown. To keep pitas warm, wrap them in a kitchen towel and place in a plastic bag or basket.

Seared Halloumi Cheese with Roasted Strawberries & Mint

4 TO 6 SERVINGS

Fried cheese. Need I say more? Sweet and salty, chewy and warm, this is the best of appetizers. Truth be told, it began as an after-school snack for our kids and then morphed into a cocktail-hour treat for adults. Halloumi, a semisoft sheep's milk cheese from Cyprus, browns up beautifully in a hot frying pan. It's exceptional with something sweet like this oven-roasted strawberry jam (don't skip the chile flakes, as they add great depth of flavor without too much heat). The cheese is firm enough to pick up as finger food, so there's no need for crackers.

1 pound small strawberries (about 2½ cups), stemmed, quartered (use Albion or Chandler, if available)

½ cup sugar

Dried red chile flakes

Flaky sea salt

8 ounces halloumi cheese, sliced into ½ inch–thick rectangles

1 tablespoon extra-virgin olive oil

10 to 12 mint leaves, torn

Preheat the oven to 375°F. Toss berries with sugar, a pinch of chile flakes, and a pinch of salt in a small, high-sided baking dish, like a large round cazuela, or a Pyrex dish approximately 9 x 11 inches. Roast until juices have reduced by half, stirring occasionally, 25 to 30 minutes. Cool. (*Jam can be made 3 days ahead. Cover and refrigerate.*)

Preheat the oven to 200°F. Drain the cheese of any extra liquid (it's typically packed in a bit of water). Pat the cheese dry.

Heat a large nonstick skillet over medium-high heat until hot. Add 1 tablespoon oil and heat for 1 minute. Add the cheese slices to the hot pan (you might have to do this in batches, as you don't want to crowd the pan). Cook until golden brown on bottom, about 5 minutes. Using a spatula, turn the cheese over and cook until soft on the inside and a little crispy on the outside. Keep warm in the oven on a heat-proof plate until you are ready to serve.

Drizzle the jam over the warm cheese. Sprinkle with mint and serve.

MARKET NOTE: In the spring, I'm constantly looking for more ways to utilize our local strawberry production. Be sure to seek out small, ripe strawberries—large strawberries often have a massive white interior that can turn the jam a brownish color when cooked.

Marinated Baby Artichokes with White Wine

4 TO 6 SERVINGS

Whether they are popping up in your yard or at the farmers market, artichokes are certainly one of the many markers in Santa Barbara that spring has arrived. Globe artichokes are perennial thistles that pop up every year in our spring garden. Each plant will have a large lead flower, which I lop off and simply boil whole and serve with Garden Hummus dip (page 149). The remaining flowers on the plant are considered baby artichokes, which are smaller, tender, and perfect for sautéing. No matter how many flowers the plant casts, come time to harvest, I always leave a few on the plant to flower—my offering to the bees.

This preparation is wonderful because the artichokes can be made in advance and served as a yummy snack alone, or as part of a crudité platter, or tossed into salads or pastas. The prepared artichokes will last for up to a week in the fridge.

2 large lemons	2 small chile de árbol
10 to 12 baby artichokes	2 fresh bay leaves
⅓ cup extra-virgin olive oil	1 teaspoon Diamond Crystal kosher salt
6 fresh thyme sprigs	½ teaspoon freshly ground pepper
4 garlic cloves, thinly sliced	⅔ cup dry white wine

Fill a large bowl with ice water; cut one lemon in half and squeeze it into the water. Using a vegetable peeler, remove the peel from the other lemon, cut the lemon in half; reserve the peel and the halved lemon.

Peel off the outer leaves of 1 artichoke in a downward motion (the leaves will snap off cleanly), until you reach a layer where the leaves are light green, almost yellow. Cut off ½ inch of the tip of the remaining artichoke top, which is pointy and sharp. Peel and trim the stem end, leaving about 1½ to 2 inches. Cut the artichoke lengthwise in half and place in the bowl of lemony water to prevent browning. Repeat with the remaining artichokes.

Drain the artichokes, then pat dry with a kitchen towel. Toss them with olive oil in a large bowl and place them cut side down in a large sauté pan (one with a fitted lid), adding any oil left behind in the bowl. Cook over medium-high heat until the artichokes begin to sizzle and turn golden brown, 7 to 8 minutes. Next, add thyme, garlic, chile, reserved lemon peel, bay leaves, salt, and pepper. Squeeze in the juice from the reserved lemon, and then add the wine and stir to incorporate. Partially cover and simmer until the tip of a sharp knife easily pierces the artichoke stems, 10 to 15 minutes, depending on the size of the artichokes.

Drain the artichokes, reserving and cooling the cooking liquid if making ahead. (*Artichokes can be made 1 week ahead. Store refrigerated in a container with their cooking liquid, to keep the artichokes from drying out. Drain before serving.*)

Serve artichokes warm, cold, or at room temperature.

Deviled Eggs with Fried Capers & Smoked Paprika

MAKES 12 DEVILED EGGS

I'm a purist when it comes to a deviled egg—the simpler the better—but the addition of the fried capers creates a crunchy texture with a briny pop. My chickens are in full production in the spring, and I find that nothing gets through a clutch of eggs like an Easter party.

1 teaspoon nonpareil capers (the little ones packed in brine)

¼ cup grapeseed oil

6 hard-boiled eggs, shells removed

3 rounded tablespoons mayonnaise

1 rounded teaspoon Dijon mustard

Flaky sea salt

Smoked paprika

Dry capers lightly with a paper towel. Cover the bottom of an 8-inch skillet with oil and place over medium-high heat. Add 1 caper bud to the pan (oil is hot enough and ready for frying when the bud in the pan has opened up and is crispy). Remove and sample it, then add the rest of the capers to the pan—be careful, as it will splatter a bit. Fry the capers until they open and look like flowers and are toasty and light brown, about 3 minutes. Transfer capers to clean paper towels to absorb excess oil.

Slice each egg in half lengthwise and carefully remove the yolk. Transfer yolks to a sieve or fine-mesh strainer and push them through using the back of a spoon or spatula. Add the mayonnaise and mustard to the yolk mixture and stir to combine. Season with salt. *(Can be made 4 hours ahead. Cover the halved whites and the yolk mixture separately and refrigerate.)*

When ready to serve, spoon the yolk mixture into the halved whites. I prefer a more rustic and casual vibe, but if you're going for elegance, use a piping bag fit with a large tip and squeeze the yolk mixture into each of the eggs.

Sprinkle with a scant pinch of the smoked paprika (don't skip the smoked paprika!) and a few of those fried capers.

Tip: For a crowd, if I am serving a variety of appetizers, I plan on two of these per person.

Spring Pea Soup with Dill Labneh

6 SERVINGS

The bright color of this pea soup is an announcement in itself that winter is over. This soup is layered with flavor and epitomizes the green, sprouting shoots of spring. Truth be told, I tend not to grow shelling peas in the garden because I always seem to miss the correct harvest time, and the potentially sweet jewels turn starchy and dry tasting. For this recipe, I buy perfectly picked peas from the farmers market or use frozen organic peas, which do not disappoint and are always in my freezer. Frozen peas are excellent for this recipe and a great timesaver compared with their fresh counterparts. If you do grow peas or buy them fresh at the farmers market, you will need four pounds of unshelled peas.

DILL LABNEH

1 cup labneh or plain Greek yogurt

2 teaspoons finely grated lemon zest (from 2 lemons)

2 teaspoons chopped fresh dill

Diamond Crystal kosher salt

SOUP

2 tablespoons extra-virgin olive oil

½ cup chopped fennel bulb (about 1 small; fronds reserved for garnish)

½ cup chopped leek (white and pale green parts only; about 1 medium)

½ cup chopped shallots (about 2 medium)

6 cups No-Stir Chicken Stock (see recipe, page 272) or other good-quality chicken stock

4 cups shelled fresh or frozen peas (about 20 ounces)

2 tablespoons (¼ stick) cold butter

2 teaspoons fresh lemon juice (from ½ lemon)

Diamond Crystal kosher salt and freshly ground pepper

Edible flowers from the garden (optional)

FOR LABNEH: Mix labneh, lemon, and dill in a bowl. Season with salt. *(Can be made 2 days ahead. Cover and refrigerate until ready to serve.)*

FOR SOUP: Heat oil in a heavy large saucepan or Dutch oven over medium heat. Add fennel, leek, and shallots and sauté until soft and translucent, about 10 minutes (be careful not to brown). Add stock and bring to a boil. Mix in all but 1 cup peas (reserved peas will be used as a garnish). Simmer soup for 10 minutes, then add butter and lemon juice.

Purée soup using an immersion blender (or a regular blender, in batches) until completely smooth. Season to taste with salt and pepper. Strain soup through a mesh strainer. *(Soup can be made 1 day ahead. Cool, cover, and refrigerate.)*

Bring soup to simmer and ladle into bowls. Top with a dollop of labneh, sprinkle with peas, and garnish with reserved fennel fronds and flowers, if available.

Simplest Garden Greens

4 TO 6 SERVINGS

To be honest, I serve this salad, or a version of it, with just about every dinner I make. It's simple and clean, and it makes great use of the lush produce we are growing. Beautiful, fresh-cut greens can stand alone. Add a little sea salt and lemon and you're already on your way to a great salad, side dish, or starter. Use mâche, wild arugula, or watercress, or a mixture of the three.

To wash the greens, grab a bowl and fill it with cold water, then dunk in the greens and gently move them around so all the excess dirt and critters come off. As for drying the greens, grab a dish towel, place the washed greens in the center, and fold the four corners up to create a makeshift satchel. Here's the fun part (and a great way to get your kids involved)—swing the satchel around and around in circles. The centrifugal force will dry the greens and also spray water all over the place, so take this fun step outside.

Keep the greens in the moist towel and store in the fridge until you are ready for mealtime. They will crisp up while in there and be nice and chilled for your salad.

6 cups wild arugula, mâche, or watercress
    (lightly packed; about 5 ounces), chilled
1 small lemon, cut in half
½ teaspoon flaky sea salt

⅓ cup extra-virgin olive oil
Parmesan shavings (optional)
Freshly ground pepper

Put the greens in a large bowl and squeeze the juice from the lemon over the top. Add the salt and toss with your hands, making sure you get full coverage on the greens. Next, drizzle with the oil and top with parmesan (if using) and mix again. Hit it with some ground black pepper and more sea salt.

Little Gem Wedge with Garden Goddess

Inspired by the classic dressing but built for a modern crowd, this is a vegan version of a green goddess, sans anchovy or dairy, and it's a fantastic way to use the last of your garden herbs of the season. You can count on someone in the crowd to be vegan, and it's nice to have options that just taste good no matter what your restrictions might be. This dressing is also great as a dip with raw veggies and makes a beautiful coleslaw mixed with thinly sliced napa cabbage (hello, St. Patrick's Day!).

Crispy and sweet, the little gem is a smaller version of romaine lettuce. Cut it in half and it's a perfect portion for a side salad.

GARDEN GODDESS
½ cup (packed) fresh cilantro leaves and stems
⅓ cup (packed) fresh mint leaves
⅓ cup (packed) fresh parsley leaves
¼ cup water
2 large garlic cloves
1 teaspoon Diamond Crystal kosher salt
1 ripe avocado, halved
3 tablespoons fresh lemon juice (from 1 lemon)
3 tablespoons unseasoned rice vinegar
¼ cup extra-virgin olive oil
¼ cup safflower oil

SALAD
6 heads little gem lettuce
2 ripe avocados, sliced
5 radishes, sliced
1 spring onion, sliced
Additional fresh herbs (with their flowers, if available)

FOR GARDEN GODDESS: Add herbs, water, garlic, and salt to a blender (a Vitamix is awesome here) and blend until the ingredients are puréed. Next, add avocado, lemon juice, and vinegar and blitz it again. With the blender running, slowly pour in the oils. Season with salt and pepper. (Dressing can be made 1 day ahead; cover and refrigerate.)

FOR SALAD: Slice the gem lettuce in half and remove the dense core by cutting a "V" shape through the heart of the stem. This will keep the wedge intact while removing the tough stem. Rinse lettuce in cold water. Shake out excess water and let dry cut side down on kitchen towels for about 5 minutes. Wrap them in the same towel, putting the two halves together, and chill in the fridge until you are ready to serve, or up to 1 day.

Arrange the hearts cut side up on a platter and drizzle with dressing. Garnish with avocado, radishes, spring onion, fresh herbs, or any flowering herbs from the garden.

KITCHEN NOTE: Try to buy oils at shops that have a high turnover. In some stores, inventory sits on the shelves and turns rancid faster than you might realize. Even your own stash can deteriorate quickly. If you're unsure how old your oil is, simply taste it. There's nothing more disappointing than utilizing fresh herbs from the garden and ruining them with bad pantry ingredients. Believe me, I know from experience!

Ridgeback Prawn Chopped Salad with Spicy Thousand Island

6 SERVINGS

I think of this as a modern-day throwback to those shrimp Louie salads of my youth. If you can't find Ridgeback prawns (they are a favorite at our farmers market in the spring), you can substitute another small, tender, peeled shrimp, like rock shrimp.

4 heads red butter lettuce, butter crunch, or Boston bibb

2 tablespoons extra-virgin olive oil

2 tablespoons (¼ stick) unsalted butter

2 tablespoons minced green garlic stalks (white and pale green parts only; about 2 stalks)

1½ pounds Ridgeback prawns, peeled, deveined, tails removed

¼ cup dry white wine

3 tablespoons chopped fresh Italian parsley, divided

1 cup halved cherry tomatoes

2 avocados, cut into large 1½-inch dice

2 teaspoons chopped fresh tarragon

Spicy Thousand Island (see recipe, page 262)

Remove the outside floppy parts of the lettuce heads so you have nice, tight balls. Cut the stems to remove any brownish color. Dunk the heads in a clean sink or bowl filled with cool water and swish around to clean. Place lettuce heads upside down on clean kitchen towels to remove any excess water. Cut the lettuce into large 2-inch pieces and wrap in a dish towel; refrigerate until you are ready to compose the salad.

In a large skillet over medium-high heat, add oil and butter; cook until the butter foams. Add the green garlic and stir to combine (be careful not to burn the garlic or it will make everything bitter tasting). Next, add the prawns; shake the pan and stir gently with a wooden spoon. Sauté until prawns are just cooked, about 2 minutes, then add wine and 1 tablespoon parsley. Season to taste with salt and pepper, then remove the shrimp—this whole process takes only about 3 minutes.

Toss the lettuce and tomatoes with enough dressing to taste. Top with avocado and shrimp, remaining 2 tablespoons parsley, and the tarragon.

Golden Beets & Blood Oranges with Citrus Vinaigrette

6 TO 8 SERVINGS

Golden beets are typically a little sweeter and milder in flavor than their red counterpart, and they marry beautifully with tart, robust-tasting blood oranges. The citrus vinaigrette here complements the earthy beets without overpowering their amazing flavor. When selecting beets at the store, look for bunches with the leaves still attached. Here are a few reasons why: #1: If the leaves look fresh, chances are the beets are newer to the shelf. #2: Beet greens are super nutritious and can be made into Minty Ginger Green Juice (page 204), or Swiss Chard Chips (page 267). #3: The greens are versatile and can be used in lieu of chard in most recipes. Basically, you're getting two veggies for the price of one, allowing more in your budget for, say, buying wine!

CITRUS VINAIGRETTE
½ cup extra-virgin olive oil
2 tablespoons white balsamic vinegar
2 tablespoons fresh blood orange juice (from 1 small orange)
1 tablespoon lemon juice (from ½ small lemon)
1 teaspoon Diamond Crystal kosher salt
½ teaspoon freshly ground pepper

SALAD
6 to 8 medium golden beets, tops removed, beets scrubbed clean
6 blood oranges
2 cups lightly packed watercress or mâche (about 2 ounces)
Flaky sea salt and freshly ground pepper
Torn fresh mint leaves

FOR VINAIGRETTE: Add all ingredients to a mason jar and shake to blend. (*Vinaigrette can be made 1 day ahead. Cover and refrigerate.*)

FOR SALAD: Boil beets in boiling water until the tip of a small sharp knife easily pierces the center, about 30 minutes. Cool the beets slightly, then peel by rubbing with a paper towel and cut each into 6 wedges. Transfer beets to a bowl.

On a cutting board with a juice groove, use a sharp paring knife to cut off the top and bottom of each orange. Starting at the top, cut off the peel and the pith (the spongy white stuff lining the inside of the rind) by slicing it away from the fruit in a downward motion. Cut the peeled oranges into ½-inch-thick slices; place in a bowl with any reserved juices from the cutting board. The juice will help keep the slices from drying out, and any extra can be used to make the dressing. (*Beets and oranges can be made 6 hours ahead; cover separately and refrigerate.*)

Toss the beets and greens with a little vinaigrette. Arrange the beets and greens in a shallow bowl or platter (this helps keep the colors distinct) and tuck in the orange slices. If you toss the beets with the oranges, your salad will be all red and you won't be able to decipher the ingredients. Taste for seasoning and add more dressing, if needed. Season with salt and pepper and sprinkle with mint.

KITCHEN NOTE: Blood oranges can stain clothing and cutting boards. Make sure to fasten up your apron strings before tackling this salad and have plenty of clean dish towels on hand. It's a messy job, but pays in delightful dividends!

Creamy Risotto with Peas

6 SERVINGS

This meal often happens on warm spring nights when friends and their kids come over for the first swim of the season. We typically end up wrapped in towels and standing around the kitchen island drinking wine, and it inevitably turns into dinner. My friend Justine calls it "Island Living." I can whip up this risotto without a recipe or a trip to the store, using what I have on hand in the pantry and freezer. It's delicious, satisfying, and a crowd-pleaser—vegetarian teens and picky kids included. The key to making great risotto is the quality of the stock and rice; with only a handful of ingredients in the recipe, be sure to use the best.

If you have fresh peas in the garden, put your friends to work to shell them while you are stirring the risotto. Frozen peas are blanched, and I find that fresh peas, if picked at the right time, don't need any blanching— the residual heat from the hot rice will heat the peas in the most perfect way.

8 cups No-Stir Chicken Stock (see recipe, page 272) or other good-quality chicken stock

3 tablespoons extra-virgin olive oil, plus more for finishing

½ cup finely chopped shallot (about 3 small shallots)

2 cups Superfino Carnaroli rice

½ cup dry white wine

2 cups fresh English peas or frozen organic petite peas (unthawed)

¼ cup (½ stick) butter, chilled, cut into 4 pieces

1 cup freshly grated parmesan, divided

I always like to place shallow heat-proof bowls in a low oven (150°F) before starting the risotto. Place stock in a large pot and bring to a boil. While the stock is heating, heat 3 tablespoons oil in a Dutch oven or large-bottomed, high-sided pan over medium heat. Add the shallots and sauté until translucent, 3 to 5 minutes. Next, increase the heat to medium-high and add the rice, stirring to incorporate. Continue to sauté until the rice begins to toast and turns translucent, about 5 minutes. Add the wine and stir until totally evaporated, about 1 minute.

Using a large ladle, add 1 ladleful of stock and stir constantly until almost absorbed. Keep adding more stock by ladlefuls, reducing the liquid in the pan by three quarters before adding more. Toward the end of cooking it will seem really soupy, but just keep stirring. This whole process takes about 15 to 20 minutes. If your arm hurts or you need to refill your drink, recruit a helper to stir for you. Once all of the stock has been added, turn off the heat. (The starch from the rice combined with the stirring and the heat will make the risotto creamy.) Add the fresh or frozen peas and the cold butter, then stir again to heat through. Mix in ½ cup of the grated parmesan. Portion risotto out into the warmed bowls. Sprinkle with remaining parmesan and add a drizzle of olive oil.

RAJ TELLS ME... A white burgundy or crisp Chardonnay from California (not oaky or buttery, please and thank you). Good choices include Pierre Yves Colin Bourgogne Blanc from Burgundy and the Sandhi Chardonnay from Sta. Rita Hills.

Campanelle Gratin with Ham & Braised Fennel

6 SERVINGS

This recipe started off Belgian and ended up Italian—story of my life, really. Growing up, my mom often made braised endive wrapped in French ham and baked in a béchamel sauce with cheese. Braised endive is on the no-fly list in my family, so I tried it with fennel and my people liked it. Once I added pasta, I had a one-pot meal that everyone loved. There are a few steps, but all are worth it—you can do the dishes once you have it in the oven.

BRAISED FENNEL

6 cups water

4 small fennel bulbs, sliced

¼ cup sweet Marsala wine

2 fresh bay leaves

1 tablespoon Diamond Crystal kosher salt

SAUCE

¼ cup (½ stick) unsalted butter

¼ cup all-purpose flour

2 cups cooking stock from braised fennel

1 8-ounce container mascarpone cheese

1 cup grated gruyère cheese

½ teaspoon Diamond Crystal kosher salt

¼ teaspoon ground white pepper

ASSEMBLY

1 tablespoon Diamond Crystal kosher salt

8 ounces (4 cups) dried Campanelle pasta

6 ounces ham steak, cut into ½-inch dice

½ cup panko breadcrumbs

¼ cup freshly grated parmesan

1 tablespoon extra-virgin olive oil

FOR FENNEL: Place water, fennel, Marsala, bay leaves, and salt in a 4-quart saucepan and bring to a boil. Reduce heat and simmer until the fennel is tender, about 15 minutes. Strain the fennel, reserving 2 cups of the cooking stock. Set braised fennel aside.

FOR SAUCE: In another heavy large saucepan, melt the butter over medium-low heat. Add the flour and stir until fragrant and golden brown, 3 to 5 minutes—be careful not to burn it! Gradually whisk in the reserved fennel cooking stock. Bring the mixture to a boil and cook until thickened, whisking until your arm hurts, about 5 to 8 minutes. Next, add the mascarpone, gruyère, salt, and pepper, and stir for a few minutes to incorporate. Set sauce aside.

FOR ASSEMBLY: Preheat the oven to 350°F. Butter a large cazuela or oven-safe earthenware cooking vessel. Bring a large pot of water with 1 tablespoon salt to a boil. Add pasta and only partially cook for 4 minutes, stirring occasionally (the pasta will be very al dente but perfectly cooked after it comes out of the oven). Drain the pasta. Mix braised fennel, sauce, pasta, and ham together in the buttered cazuela. Cover with the panko and parmesan, then drizzle with oil. Bake until the top is golden brown and the pasta is bubbling, 35 to 40 minutes.

RAJ TELLS ME... Because this dish is creamy, drink it with a white Rhône style of wine. Good ones include Jean Louis Chave Selection St. Joseph "Circa" from the Rhone or Kunin "Pape Star" from Santa Ynez Valley.

Spring Egg & Sausage Bake

6 TO 8 SERVINGS

This dish was made every Easter by my Calabrese grandmother, Nanny, when we were loaded up to our rabbit ears with dyed hard-boiled eggs. Originally, it was prepared in a pie crust, but over the years, in an attempt at lighter fare (not sure how light sausage and eggs and cheese can get?!), we ditched the crust and made it more like a frittata baked into earthenware. This dish is a fantastic one to have in your repertoire. Not only is it utterly delicious and super flavorful, it's also incredibly versatile. You can serve it as a gluten-free appetizer, cut it into square small-size bites, or bake it in a pie dish and serve with a green salad as a family-night main course.

6 hard-boiled large eggs, thinly sliced	½ cup milk
1 pound sweet Italian sausage, cooked and sliced in coins	2 teaspoons Dijon mustard
1 12-ounce log mozzarella cheese, thinly sliced	1 teaspoon Diamond Crystal kosher salt
6 large eggs	¼ teaspoon cayenne pepper
	¼ cup freshly grated parmesan

Preheat the oven to 350°F. Butter a 9-inch round or 8-inch square baking dish. Place each of your ingredients (sliced eggs, sliced sausage, and sliced cheese) in bowls so you have an assembly line ready to go. Layer ⅓ of the hard-boiled eggs on the bottom of the baking dish, followed by ⅓ of the sausage and ⅓ of the mozzarella. Repeat, creating layers like a lasagna until your ingredients are all used.

Crack the raw eggs into a large bowl and whisk until completely blended. Add the milk, mustard, salt, and cayenne pepper and whisk to incorporate. Pour over the layered mixture in the baking dish, then top with an even layer of parmesan. (*Can be made 6 hours ahead; cover tightly and refrigerate.*)

Bake uncovered until the eggs are set, 30 to 35 minutes (add 5 minutes more if refrigerated). Cool slightly. Serve warm or at room temperature.

RAJ TELLS ME... Eggs can be tricky to pair with wine, but since it's an Italian dish, a light, crisp, floral white wine like an Arneis from Piedmont would work well. Suggestions include Vietti Arneis from Piedmont and Palmina Arneis from Santa Ynez Valley.

Oven-Baked Ribs with Nasturtium Gremolata

4 TO 6 SERVINGS

Crispy on the outside and succulent on the inside, these ribs are so simple to make. I take any opportunity to use nasturtiums when they hit the scene in spring. Their rigorous growth of lush foliage and bright orange flowers blanket the garden like no other. They are delicious in the gremolata, but if you don't have them on hand, substitute with arugula. Or skip the gremolata altogether and just serve the ribs with a side of Homemade Barbecue Sauce (page 265), but don't skip the Mustardy Potatoes & Celery (page 67).

NASTURTIUM GREMOLATA
½ cup (packed) nasturtium leaves and flowers, finely chopped
¼ cup finely chopped fresh Italian parsley
1 teaspoon grated orange zest (from 1 small orange)
1 teaspoon grated lemon zest (from 1 small lemon)
1 large garlic clove, grated

RIBS
2 racks pork baby back ribs

1 tablespoon Diamond Crystal kosher salt
1 tablespoon whole cumin seeds, toasted and ground
1 tablespoon dried Aleppo pepper (see Spice Drawer, page 274) or chile powder
1 tablespoon sumac (see Spice Drawer, page 274)
2 teaspoons freshly ground pepper
2 teaspoons smoked paprika

Homemade Barbecue Sauce (optional) (see recipe, page 265)

FOR GREMOLATA: Mix all ingredients in a bowl. *(Can be made 4 hours ahead. Cover and refrigerate.)*

FOR RIBS: Preheat the oven to 450°F. Place the ribs on a large rimmed baking sheet. Pat the ribs dry with clean towels (paper or cloth) and season both sides of the meat with 1 tablespoon salt. Mix cumin, Aleppo, sumac, pepper, and paprika in a small bowl. Rub the spice mixture all over the ribs. Cook the hell out of them for 45 minutes. The result will be tender meat and crispy skin.

Sprinkle ribs with gremolata. Serve with barbecue sauce, if desired.

RAJ TELLS ME... A medium-bodied red wine like a grenache will carry the spices. Consider Comando G Garnacha "La Bruja de Rozas" from Madrid or "A Tribute to Grace" Grenache, Santa Barbara County.

Leg of Lamb Stuffed with Feta & Oregano

6 TO 8 SERVINGS

Oregano is often overlooked and underused in the kitchen. Its emerald leaves are not only pretty, but amazingly flavorful. Here, it's tossed with garlic and feta and used as a stuffing for lamb in a succulent Mediterranean-style main course. Related to the mint family, oregano is just as prolific in the garden as mint. I like to hang flowering sprigs of oregano upside down on a hook in my kitchen to dry and use later in sauces or on pizza.

1 4-pound boneless leg of lamb

⅓ cup garlic cloves

1 tablespoon Diamond Crystal kosher salt

¼ cup fresh oregano leaves, plus more for garnish

½ teaspoon dried red chile flakes

1 tablespoon extra-virgin olive oil

⅔ cup crumbled feta or ricotta salata

1 tablespoon grapeseed oil

Spring onions, sliced (optional)

Open the leg of lamb and dry it on both sides with clean towels. Place lamb boned side up on a rimmed baking sheet. In a mortar and pestle, pound the garlic and salt, then add ¼ cup oregano and chile flakes and continue to pulverize until a paste forms. Stir in olive oil. Spread this mixture over the inside of the lamb, then sprinkle with the feta. Starting at the narrow end, roll up lamb tightly, enclosing filling. Tie with kitchen string at 2-inch intervals to hold shape. Pat lamb dry. *(Can be made 1 day ahead. Let stand 2 hours at room temperature before roasting.)*

Preheat the oven to 325°F. Pat the outside of the lamb dry of any moisture and season with salt and pepper. In a large cast-iron skillet on medium-high heat add the oil (I use grapeseed oil because it has a higher smoke point for the hot temperature needed to sear the meat) and watch for it to dance or move around the skillet. Add the roast to the skillet and brown evenly on all sides, using tongs to turn, about 8 to 10 minutes total. Once the lamb has been seared, place on a rack in a roasting pan. Roast lamb until an instant-read thermometer inserted into the thickest part registers 135°F for medium-rare, about 1¼ hours (or about 18 minutes per pound).

Let the lamb rest at least 30 minutes before slicing, and don't forget to remove the string! Slice lamb thinly and garnish with spring onions and fresh oregano leaves.

RAJ TELLS ME... Lamb always loves Syrah—it's a classic pairing. We like Domaine Auguste Clape Cornas "Renaissance" from the Rhone or Piedrasassi P.S. Syrah from Santa Barbara County.

Blistered Asparagus with Pistachios, Green Garlic & Chives

6 SERVINGS

I have tried numerous times to grow asparagus in our garden, but after devoting a good deal of space, lots of water, and tons of time only to get a few thin and measly stalks, I decided to scrap our crop and shop for it at the farmers market.

Garlic, on the other hand, is easy to grow in our Santa Barbara climate and is a very rewarding crop, as it delivers products in so many ways. #1: Pick it early for delicious and lovely green garlic. #2: Pull it from the earth once the leaves have browned for a full head. #3: Take a clove from the fully dried head and plant it for the process to repeat. It's the simplest "Lather. Rinse. Repeat." of gardening.

To pick the best asparagus wherever you shop, look for stalks that are thick and flower tops that are tight like a ball—not sprouting or stringy.

5 tablespoons extra-virgin olive oil, divided

¼ cup thinly sliced green garlic (from 1 to 2 green garlic heads with about an inch of the green stem)

1 teaspoon grated lemon zest (from 1 small lemon)

½ cup toasted salted pistachios, coarsely chopped

2 bunches asparagus, ends trimmed, stalks cut on bias into 2-inch pieces

½ teaspoon Diamond Crystal kosher salt

1 tablespoon chopped fresh chives

1 teaspoon fresh lemon juice (from ½ lemon)

Flaky sea salt and freshly cracked pepper

Lemon wedges

Chive blossoms (optional)

Preheat the broiler, positioning the oven rack about 5 inches from the heat source.

Stir 3 tablespoons oil, green garlic, and lemon zest in a small saucepan over medium heat until fragrant and warm, about 3 minutes. Mix in toasted nuts and set aside.

Place the asparagus on a rimmed baking sheet. Drizzle with 2 tablespoons oil and ½ teaspoon salt; toss to coat. Broil for 2 minutes. Pull out the baking sheet to check on how things are going (be careful not to burn the asparagus) and shake the pan. Continue broiling the asparagus until the tips begin to turn golden brown, about 8 more minutes, shaking the asparagus every 2 to 3 minutes.

Add the pistachio mixture, chives, and lemon juice to the asparagus and toss to coat. Place the asparagus on a platter and pour any residual sauce from the sheet pan over the top. Season with salt and pepper. Garnish with lemon wedges. Serve warm or at room temperature and garnish with chive blossoms, if available.

KITCHEN NOTE: Try this recipe with sugar snap peas instead of asparagus and get a similarly tasty result. Feel free to play around with different spring herbs, such as thyme, savory, or mint. Go easy with the lemon—just a touch of it brightens the flavors in this simple dish, but too much will quickly overwhelm the gentle green garlic.

Quick Sautéed Sugar Snap Peas with Tangerine

4 TO 6 SERVINGS

My family loves sugar snap peas and a veggie we can all agree on is a good thing! They are so naturally sweet, you really don't need to do much to them to make them flavorful; in fact, I feel the less you cook them, the sweeter the veggie remains.

If the peas are large, slice them in half on the bias to keep the integrity of the pea husk shape. If your peas are smaller, you don't need to slice at all. When you clean the strings off, pinch the crown top and gently snap the top off and pull down toward the bottom of the pea. If you do it right, you'll get both strings off the pod with one movement.

2 tablespoons extra-virgin olive oil

½ cup thinly sliced shallots (about 2 medium)

1 pound sugar snap peas, strings removed

1 teaspoon fresh thyme leaves, plus more for garnish

½ teaspoon Diamond Crystal kosher salt

¼ teaspoon freshly cracked pepper

3 tablespoons fresh tangerine juice (from 1 large tangerine)

1 tablespoon brandy or cognac

½ teaspoon Aleppo pepper (see Spice Drawer, page 274)

2 tangerines, peeled, sectioned

Heat oil in a large, heavy skillet over medium-high heat until hot. Add shallots and sauté until translucent, about 3 minutes. Next, add sugar snap peas, 1 teaspoon thyme, salt, and pepper. Sauté until the skin on the peas begins to blister, about 3 minutes. Once cooked, remove the sugar snap peas to a plate. Add the juice and brandy to the skillet and boil until reduced by half, about 1 minute. Return the peas to the skillet and toss to reheat. Transfer peas to a platter. Sprinkle with Aleppo pepper and tangerine segments. Garnish with thyme leaves and serve.

Grilled King Trumpet Mushrooms with Sherry Marinade

4-6 SERVINGS

Once daylight savings begins, it's open season for grilling. I work in tandem with my husband—he mans the meat and I (wo)man the mushrooms. It feels like a celebration to be outside together. King Trumpets are meaty and delicious mushrooms to grill. I often find great wild mushroom varieties at Asian markets. They are often as reasonably priced as they are delicious. Note that a little marinade goes a long way with mushrooms.

20 ounces King Trumpet mushrooms

½ cup extra-virgin olive oil

⅓ cup dry sherry

3 garlic cloves, smashed

1 tablespoon plus ¼ teaspoon chopped fresh rosemary

1 teaspoon grated lemon zest (from 1 lemon)

1 teaspoon freshly cracked pepper

Diamond Crystal kosher salt

Flaky sea salt

Cut bottom ¼ inch off of each mushroom. Cut each mushroom lengthwise into thirds, keeping the shape of the mushroom. Place mushrooms in a large baking dish.

Whisk oil, sherry, garlic, 1 tablespoon rosemary, lemon zest, and pepper in a small bowl. Pour the marinade over the mushrooms; turn to coat. Let the mushrooms marinate for at least 20 minutes or up to 2 hours.

Prepare the grill (medium-high heat). Arrange the mushrooms in a single layer directly on the grill (or in a perforated grill pan). Season generously with kosher salt. Grill mushrooms until caramelized on both sides and easily pierced with a knife, turning once or twice, about 5 minutes. Before serving, sprinkle with sea salt and ¼ teaspoon rosemary.

Mustardy Potatoes & Celery

4 TO 6 SERVINGS

Two things grow prolifically in my garden without much effort at all: potatoes and celery—score for us, my family loves both. Both seem pedestrian but carry the most unique flavor when grown in the yard. The first time I grew potatoes, the girls were toddlers, and digging for them was like searching for buried treasure. Seriously, it was one of the most memorable activities from their youth. Potatoes should be hard and unblemished. I never peel them because the skin is so thin it just dissolves, and I like the earthiness it carries through the recipe.

1½ pounds small baby Yukon Gold or fingerling potatoes

2 garlic cloves

1 fresh bay leaf

1½ teaspoons Diamond Crystal kosher salt, divided

¼ cup extra-virgin olive oil

1 tablespoon white balsamic vinegar

1 tablespoon white wine vinegar

1 tablespoon grainy mustard

1 teaspoon Dijon mustard

½ teaspoon freshly ground pepper

3 celery stalks, diced (reserve any tender leaves)

2 tablespoons minced shallot (about 1 small shallot)

6 cornichon pickles, diced (optional)

Pierce each potato with a paring knife and place them with the garlic and bay leaf in a pot. Add enough cold water to cover by 2 inches. Add ½ teaspoon salt and bring the water to a boil. Reduce heat to a simmer and cook until almost tender, about 10 minutes.

While the potatoes cook, whisk oil, vinegars, mustards, 1 teaspoon salt, and pepper in a large serving bowl—no sense in doing more dishes than you need to. Mix in celery, shallot, and cornichons, if using.

When the potatoes are almost tender, drain them in a colander. I like them a little underdone at this point because they will continue to cook after you drain them. Fish out one of the garlic cloves and mash (it will be warm and soft). Add the mashed garlic to the dressing and stir to incorporate. Cut each potato in half (they will be hot to the touch) and immediately add to the prepared dressing. Give them all a good mix. Continue to mix the potato salad occasionally as it cools. Serve at room temperature.

Crispy Ghee Fried Potatoes with Fresh Bay & Aioli

4 TO 6 SERVINGS

These potatoes are crispy on the outside and soft in the middle. I steam them first, which can be done up to a day in advance and then finish them in a sauté pan before eating. Using ghee in this recipe makes the potatoes extra crisp, so seek some out before you try substitutions. If you love to cook and garden, you would be well served to invest in a sweet bay tree. They are beautiful, sculptural, and drought-tolerant, providing lovely fresh leaves at your fingertips every time you cook. Who knows how old that dried bay really is in your spice drawer anyway?

1½ pounds small Russet potatoes
1 teaspoon Diamond Crystal kosher salt
3 tablespoons ghee
2 fresh bay leaves

Smoked paprika
Flaky sea salt
Aioli (see recipe, page 265)

Peel and cut the potatoes crosswise into 1-inch-thick slices. Add a few inches of water and kosher salt to a medium pot fitted with a steamer. Add potatoes and bring to a boil. Cover and steam over medium heat until potatoes soften, about 15 minutes.

Melt the ghee in a heavy large skillet over medium-high heat. Add bay leaves, then scatter the potatoes in one layer and let cook undisturbed until golden brown on bottom, about 7 minutes. Using tongs, turn potatoes over and cook undisturbed until golden brown on bottom, 5 to 7 minutes. Remove the bay leaves. Transfer potatoes to a platter. Sprinkle with smoked paprika and sea salt. Serve with Aioli.

Red Rhubarb Amaretto Torte

8 SERVINGS

This gluten-free cake is simple to put together and so pretty. You can use virtually any fruit (think apricots in the summer or figs in the fall) to sit atop, but I love the sour rhubarb, as it marries so nicely with the sweet almond-flavored cake. I grow a small patch of rhubarb in the yard, but it's not the most successful crop because it prefers a cooler climate to Santa Barbara's. Luckily, it's available at our farmers market. It's a perfect celebration of spring, and the positioning of the rhubarb on top looks like a woven basket when it's put together.

24 ounces red rhubarb, cleaned with ends trimmed, stalks sliced lengthwise in half, then cut crosswise into 1½-inch pieces

1¼ cups sugar, divided

¼ cup amaretto liqueur, plus more for drizzle

3 tablespoons fresh lime juice (from 2 limes)

5 large eggs, room temperature, separated

1¾ cups almond flour (6 ounces)

2 teaspoons grated lime zest (from 1 large lime)

½ teaspoon flaky sea salt

White sanding sugar

Preheat the oven to 350°F. Spray or butter one 9-inch square tart pan with a removable bottom, or one 10¼-inch round tart pan with a removable bottom.

In a bowl, toss the rhubarb, ½ cup sugar, ¼ cup amaretto, and lime juice. Set aside.

Grab a handheld mixer and two large bowls. In one bowl, beat the yolks with ¾ cup sugar for about 5 minutes until thick and light yellow in color, then mix in the almond flour, lime zest, and salt. Rinse off the beaters (unplug it before you do this—please and thank you) and whip up the whites in the second bowl until stiff, about 5 minutes. Add ⅓ of the whites to the yolk batter and stir to incorporate. Fold in the remaining egg whites, being careful not to overmix. Pour the batter into prepared tart pan.

Using a slotted spoon, remove rhubarb pieces from the macerating liquid (reserve liquid). Arrange rhubarb on top of the batter in a pattern—I like to arrange in a basket weave. Be creative and have fun! Sprinkle with sanding sugar. Reserve any leftover rhubarb pieces.

Bake until the torte is firm to the touch and golden brown, 30 to 35 minutes. Transfer to a rack to cool. Press pan bottom up to release torte from pan. (*Can be made 6 hours ahead. Cover and let stand at room temperature.*)

Tip: Cut any remaining rhubarb into small dice and add to a small skillet along with its macerating liquid. Cook over medium heat until soft and liquid has reduced, 5 to 7 minutes. Mash with a fork to create a jam-like texture and taste, adding more sugar if needed. It's great stuffed into crêpes, folded into yogurt, or stirred into a cocktail.

RAJ TELLS ME... This is great to enjoy with a vin santo, such as Felsina Vin Santo, Chianti, Tuscany, Italy.

Egg Meringues with Tangerine Curd

MAKES ABOUT 3 DOZEN MERINGUES

Our backyard chickens produce eggs with yolks that are more orange than yellow, so I thought it would be more fitting to make the curd with both tangerine and lemon juice. The sweet crunch of the meringue matched with the tangy creaminess of the curd is just wonderful.

These mini pavlovas are pretty straightforward to make, and all parts can thankfully be accomplished in advance.

TANGERINE CURD
½ cup fresh tangerine juice, strained (from 3 to 4 tangerines)
⅓ cup fresh lemon juice, strained (from 1 large lemon)
⅓ cup sugar
1 large egg and 4 large yolks
½ teaspoon flaky sea salt
½ cup (1 stick) unsalted butter, cut into pieces

MERINGUE EGGS
Vegetable oil (for brushing)
1 cup sugar
4 large egg whites, room temperature
2 teaspoons cornstarch
1 teaspoon distilled white vinegar
Flaky sea salt

FOR CURD: Whisk juices, sugar, 1 egg, yolks, and sea salt in a glass Pyrex bowl. Set over a saucepan of simmering water, add butter pieces, and cook, stirring constantly, until thickened and an instant-read thermometer inserted into the curd registers 180°F, about 10 to 12 minutes. Cover with plastic wrap, pressing the plastic onto the surface of the curd, and refrigerate until cold. *(Curd can be made 5 days ahead. Keep refrigerated.)*

FOR MERINGUES: Preheat the oven to 200°F. Line large baking sheets with parchment and brush with oil. Put the sugar, egg whites, cornstarch, and vinegar in the bowl of a stand mixer and whisk at the highest speed until soft peaks form, about 5 minutes.

Spoon the meringue into a piping bag fitted with a large tip (the 804 tip—it's big!). Pipe small 2½- to 3-inch egg-shaped ovals onto the parchment, starting with the center and moving outward, circling twice around the perimeter to create a raised frame for your "egg yolk," spacing them about 2 inches apart.

Bake for 1 hour, then turn off the oven, keeping the door closed. Allow the meringues to cool completely in the oven, about 1 hour. They will be crisp on the outside and somewhat soft on the inside. *(Meringues can be made 2 days ahead. Store meringues between sheets of waxed paper in an airtight container at room temperature.)*

Just before serving, spoon a small dollop of tangerine curd into the middle of each meringue.

RAJ TELLS ME... A Moscato d'Asti would go beautifully with this dessert.

Triple Coconut Cake

8 TO 10 SERVINGS

For special occasions, birthdays, holidays, and dinner parties, this moist coconut creation is by far my most requested cake. The cake and frosting both stem from simple, classic recipes, so they're easy to make. What truly makes it shine is the layer upon layer of unsweetened coconut ingredients that make the cake flavorful without being cloying. I decorate it with toasted unsweetened coconut and our season's first roses. Make sure the flowers you choose are both edible and unsprayed. The last thing you want to do is serve to your guests a side of chemicals and pesticides!

COCONUT CAKE

1 cup (2 sticks) unsalted butter, room temperature

2 cups sugar

4 large eggs

3 cups all-purpose flour

5 teaspoons baking powder

1 teaspoon Diamond Crystal kosher salt

1 cup canned unsweetened coconut milk

1 teaspoon pure vanilla extract

1 teaspoon coconut extract

COCONUT FILLING

1 cup plain (full fat or 2%) Greek yogurt

¾ cup shredded unsweetened coconut

⅓ cup sugar

¼ cup canned unsweetened coconut milk

8-MINUTE FROSTING

1½ cups sugar

⅓ cup coconut water, fresh, canned, or bottled

2 large egg whites

½ teaspoon Diamond Crystal kosher salt

¼ teaspoon cream of tartar

ASSEMBLY

1½ cups unsweetened coconut flakes, toasted if desired

Unsprayed roses

FOR CAKE: Preheat the oven to 350°F. Butter three 8-inch round cake pans with 2-inch-high sides; dust with flour, tapping out excess. In a mixer fitted with the paddle attachment, beat butter and sugar until light in color

BAKING NOTE: | For the most moist cakes, bake the cakes a day or up to a week in advance. Cool the cakes on a rack, wrap them well with cling film, and store them in the freezer until the day you would like to serve. I don't know the science behind this technique of freezing the cakes, but it makes them superlative! If you really want to go all out, toast the coconut flakes used to garnish the cake. Spread the coconut out in a single layer on a rimmed baking sheet and toast in a 350°F oven until golden brown, 8 to 10 minutes.

and fluffy in texture, about 5 minutes. Next, add eggs one at a time, beating just to blend after each addition and stopping occasionally to scrape down the sides of the bowl.

In a separate bowl, whisk flour, baking powder, and salt. Combine coconut milk and both extracts in a measuring cup. Add both mixtures to the bowl of the mixer, alternating the flour and milk mixtures (beginning and ending with the flour), beating until smooth. Pour batter evenly into pans. Bake until the cake pulls slightly away from the sides of the pan and a tester inserted in the center comes out clean, about 25 minutes. Cool cakes in pans on racks for 15 minutes. Run a small knife around the pan sides to loosen. Turn cakes out onto racks and cool completely.

FOR FILLING: Mix all ingredients together in a small bowl and reserve until you are ready to assemble the cakes.

FOR FROSTING: Combine all of the ingredients in a large Pyrex bowl. Using a hand-held electric mixer, beat the mixture for 1 minute, then place the bowl over a medium saucepan filled with 2 inches of boiling water (make sure the water does not touch the bottom of the bowl or your frosting will turn gritty). Beat constantly on high speed over medium-high heat for the remaining 7 minutes (if it gets too hot, remove the pan from the heat for a minute but continue beating). Cool completely.

FOR ASSEMBLY: Poke each layer of cake with a toothpick 10 times and divide the filling equally between the three. Place 1 layer on a platter. Top with the second and third layers and refrigerate at least 1 hour before frosting. (*Can be made 6 hours ahead. Keep refrigerated.*)

Spread frosting over the entire cake and then press the coconut flakes on with your hand—if you cup your hand slightly, it will hold the flakes and go onto the cake nicely. Garnish with roses.

RAJ TELLS ME... When pairing dessert with dessert wine, the sweetness levels should be similar. Try this one with a sauterne or sauterne-like wine, such as a Kracher Cuvée Beerenauslese from Austria.

Fresh Mint Chocolate Chip Ice Cream with Magic Chocolate Shell

4 SERVINGS

This is a Philadelphia-style ice cream, which means it's eggless, and couldn't be any easier to make. It's delicious on its own or you can "go big" and top it with a blanket of Magic Chocolate Shell for the ultimate indulgence.

1½ cups whipping cream

1 cup whole milk

½ cup sugar

¼ cup unsweetened cocoa powder

15 fresh peppermint leaves

Diamond Crystal kosher salt

⅓ cup coarsely chopped semisweet chocolate
   (about 2 ounces)

Magic Chocolate Shell (recipe follows)

In a heavy medium saucepan, combine cream, milk, sugar, cocoa, and mint. Add a pinch of salt. Whisk over medium heat just until the sugar has completely dissolved and the cocoa powder is incorporated. Remove from heat and cool, then refrigerate until cold, about 2 hours.

Stir the mixture and strain it into the bowl of an ice cream maker. Add the chopped chocolate and churn until thick and creamy; time will vary depending on the machine. My ice cream maker instructions say to wait to add the chocolate chunks until the last 5 minutes of churn time, but I say instructions be damned—throw in the chocolate from the start. Serve immediately or cover and store in the freezer up to 6 hours.

Scoop ice cream into bowls or glasses. Drizzle with Magic Chocolate Shell. If you choose to sprinkle a little sea salt on the top, I won't stop you!

Magic Chocolate Shell / MAKES ABOUT 1 CUP

Magic Shell made its debut on grocery store shelves in the '80s, when I donned neon T-shirts and crimped my hair. Now my girls, with a similar look, make a magic shell with three ingredients in the microwave. We love the hard shell that forms over the cold ice cream. I love adding a little tequila to the mix. It gives it a warmish oaky flavor but isn't overly boozy.

1 cup bittersweet chocolate chips (about 6 ounces)
¼ cup coconut oil

¼ teaspoon flaky sea salt
1 tablespoon tequila anejo (optional)

Combine chocolate, oil, salt, and tequila (if using) in the top of a double boiler over medium heat and stir until melted. Keep the mixture warm until ready to use. (*Can be made 5 days ahead. Cover and refrigerate. Reheat in 30-second increments in the microwave.*)

Summer

Sunshine, Stone Fruit & Sand

When I was growing up in Southern California, my mom always packed coolers of drinks and stone fruit for the beach. I equate sun-soaked, sandy summer days with tart nectarines, juicy Santa Rosa plums, and the smell of BullFrog sunblock. Today, my summer garden explodes with plump fruit: cherries, peaches, apricots, blackberries, mulberries, raspberries, and strawberries. Tomatoes are thriving, as are shishito and fresno peppers. Tomatillos, squash of all types, cucumbers, pole and bush beans, and herbs like lemon verbena, cilantro, and basil are all in season too.

At the beginning of August, our town comes together to celebrate a beloved Santa Barbara tradition: Old Spanish Days, or as it's simply known, Fiesta. It's a five-day celebration of Santa Barbara's rich cultural heritage, with church festivals, one of the nation's largest equine parades, and endless stalls of the best Mexican food. Mexican food is part of our everyday, home-cooking culture in Santa Barbara, and it's also one of my most favorite cuisines. Strawberry Mezcal Margaritas (page 91), Avocado Slaw (page 103), and Carnitas Tacos (page 116)—yes, please. In my opinion, Mexican food is the best way to show off summer produce—many of its key ingredients are at the height of flavor.

As for entertaining, summer means the kids are out of school, and we kick off the season by opening up the pool, pouring a white port and tonic (or two), and firing up the grill for Orange-Marinated Tri-Tip with Chimichurri & Padrón Peppers (page 119). We usually start summer parties by picking one good cocktail for the entire group and offering a light quaffer of a wine, like a Gamay or a Barbera, with dinner. This type of red wine on a hot summer night (and any suggestion in the chapter) is perfect to chill. Please resist, however, the temptation of putting ice cubes in your wine, which will dilute the flavor; instead, chill it in the fridge or lay the bottle on top of ice for about 30 minutes. Or consider a rosé; see the sidebar for ideas.

I love tending to my garden all year long, but nothing excites me more than tomato season. Maybe it's my summer garden memories with my grandmother, or maybe it's just that absolutely nothing is as good as eating homegrown tomatoes. A fresh-picked Brandywine tomato, warmed by the sun, sliced and simply sprinkled with flaky sea salt, is a killer accompaniment to any summer meal. Don't overthink great ingredients—simple is best. Here's to days of sunshine, stone fruit, and sand.

TIME FOR ROSÉ

It's not just your fruits and veggies that are in season—rosé is also in full swing by late spring. The best ones are light, fresh, and versatile enough to go with just about any summer meal. Here are a few of Raj's favorite rosés to get you on your way; just seek out the current vintages:

SANCERRE ROSÉ: This wine from the Loire Valley is made entirely of Pinot Noir. Typically lean, crisp, and low in alcohol—perfect for hot days of daytime drinking. Good producers include:

- DOMAINE VACHERON
- FRANÇOIS COTAT
- GÉRARD BOULAY
- FRANÇOIS CROCHET

PROVENÇAL ROSÉ: A blend of grapes from the Provence region, this versatile wine is easy-drinking and richer in style than the Sancerre. Bottlings to look for:

- DOMAINE TEMPIER BANDOL
- DOMAINE LA BASTIDE BLANCHE BANDOL
- CLOS STE MAGDELEINE CASSIS
- CHÂTEAU PEYRASSOL CÔTES DE PROVENCE

WHAT TO PLANT NOW

In Santa Barbara, mid-July is a good time to begin planting for fall. This is a primo opportunity to haul out some of the tired and less-than-lovely-looking plantings of tomatoes and zucchini to make room for soft lettuces, fresh nightshades, and brassicas.

WATERMELON RADISHES	HEAD LETTUCES: BUTTER LETTUCE & SANGUINE AMELIORE	WILD ARUGULA & DRAGON'S TONGUE	BLOOMSDALE SPINACH
CARROTS: SCARLET NANTES, CHANTENAY RED CORE, OR COSMIC PURPLE	WHITE EGG TURNIPS	CARENTAN LEEK	CINDERELLA PUMPKIN
MORE TOMATOES OF THE LARGER VARIETY: BLACK KRIM, CHEROKEE PURPLE, AND PAUL ROBESON		KABOCHA SQUASH	PURPLE SPROUT-ING BROCCOLI & ROMANESCO

Summer Recipes

Summary Drinks

4.

6.

5.

Watermelon Cooler

MAKES 6 TO 8 DRINKS

This cooler makes great use of those extra watermelon slices that end up in the fridge post-barbecue. If you want to make a cocktail out of the juice, get your hands on a good Bacanora, a mezcal-based spirit from Sonora. It's less smoky and has a wonderful earthiness that works beautifully with watermelon. Or try the cooler with your favorite spirit. It's also great with bourbon, tequila, or vodka.

4 cups 2-inch seedless watermelon chunks
    (from ½ watermelon)
2 tablespoons sugar
2 tablespoons fresh lime juice (from 1 to 2 limes)
4 cups water
Spirits, such as Bacanora, bourbon, mezcal, or tequila
    (optional)
Lime wedges (garnish)

Place watermelon, sugar, and lime juice in a large bowl. Mash the watermelon with a potato masher until crushed and juice is released. Strain into a pitcher, pressing on solids, then mix in water. Pour into glasses filled with ice (pick pretty ones). Add a splash of your favorite spirit, if desired. Garnish with lime.

Summer Sonics

MAKES 2 COCKTAILS

I hope the Brits don't mind my suggesting half tonic and half soda water for this cocktail. It's so light and delicious and has less sugar. Rum, gin, vodka, and white port all work beautifully in a sonic, but my favorite is white port, which adds a wonderful richness and is an awesome less-alcoholic option for day drinking (you're welcome). These days, most bottle shops carry a good range of organic tonics made without high-fructose corn syrup—make the switch!

4 ounces (½ cup) gin, vodka, or white port
2 ounces (¼ cup) chilled sparkling water
2 ounces (¼ cup) chilled tonic water
2 lime slices, 2 cucumber spears, 2 sprigs lemon
    verbena (garnish)
2 plum wedges and 2 orange wedges (garnish)

Fill 2 glasses with ice. Add gin, vodka, or port, sparkling water, and tonic water, dividing equally. If using gin or vodka, garnish with lime, cucumber, and lemon verbena. If using port, garnish with plum and orange wedges.

Cold-Brew Lemon Verbena Tea
(photo page 135)

Lemon verbena grows prolifically in my summer garden. It's not only a wonderfully fragrant garnish for the Summer Sonic, but it also adds such a pretty touch to floral arrangements. I keep a pitcher of this tea in my fridge in the summer months. Put 6 lemon verbena sprigs in a large pitcher and fill with cool water. Allow the brew to steep in the fridge 4 to 24 hours. Strain and serve over ice.

Basil Martini Spritz with Olives

MAKES 2 COCKTAILS

This version of a martini is perfect for a hot summer night. Served over ice and finished with sparkling water, it's herbaceous and super fresh. To make a non-alcoholic version, add twice as much of the olive juice and omit the alcohol.

5 large fresh basil leaves
4 ounces (½ cup) Koskenkorva vodka or Broker's gin (see Bar Tips & Tools, page 283)
1 ounce (2 tablespoons) olive juice (from jar of green olives)
4 ounces (½ cup) chilled sparkling water
2 lemon peel twists
4 green olives with pits, such as Castelvetrano (garnish)
2 fresh basil sprigs (garnish)

Mash basil leaves in a cocktail shaker using the end of a spoon until bruised. Fill the shaker ¾ full with ice. Add vodka and olive juice and shake vigorously. Strain into 2 glasses filled with ice and top with sparkling water. Run a lemon twist around the rim of each glass; add twists to glasses. Garnish with olives and basil sprigs.

BAR NOTE: I like to top the drinks with Agua de Piedra or Topo Chico because they have bigger bubbles than other sparkling waters. Look for them online or at some Mexican markets and specialty stores.

Heirloom Bloody Marys with Celery Salt

MAKES 2 COCKTAILS

This Bloody Mary utilizes the harvest baskets in the best possible way—just buzz fresh tomatoes and a little jalapeño and you're on your way to hair-of-the-dog heaven. My dad was always the master of Bloody Marys, making them in his hammered copper bar on Sunday mornings. He referred to them as a morning "lift."

TOMATO PURÉE
1 pound heirloom tomatoes, rinsed, quartered, stems removed
½ small jalapeño chile, seeded (optional)
1 teaspoon flaky sea salt
1 teaspoon fresh lemon juice (from ½ lemon)

COCKTAIL
2½ teaspoons celery seeds, toasted
2 teaspoons flaky sea salt
1 lime wedge
4 ounces (½ cup) vodka, such as Tito's or Koskenkorva
Tomato Purée
Lemon wheel or wedges (garnish)
Celery stalks with leaves (garnish)

FOR PURÉE: Purée tomatoes and jalapeño (if using) in a blender until smooth. Mix in 1 teaspoon salt and lemon juice. (Can be made 6 hours ahead. Cover and refrigerate.)

FOR COCKTAIL: Grind celery seeds with salt in a mortar and pestle. Pour celery salt onto a small plate. Run a lime wedge around the rim of 2 tall glasses and dip in prepared celery salt. Fill glasses with ice. Add 2 ounces vodka to each glass and fill with Tomato Purée. Garnish with lemon wheels and celery stalks.

Strawberry Mezcal Margaritas

MAKES 2 COCKTAILS

Smoky mezcal mixed with summer's sweet strawberries and a salt-spiced rim—it's a match made in cocktail heaven. Mezcal can be made from a number of different agaves and gets its smoky characteristics from agave hearts (piña) burned in underground pits.

1 tablespoon Spiced Rimming Salt (see recipe, page 271)

1 lime wedge

1 cup strawberries, hulled, cut in half

1 chile de árbol, toasted in a dry skillet

4 ounces (½ cup) mezcal Espadín, such as Vago or Pierde Almas

2 ounces (¼ cup) Cointreau

2 ounces (¼ cup) fresh orange juice (from 1 orange)

2 ounces (¼ cup) fresh lime juice (from 2 to 3 limes)

2 whole strawberries with stems (garnish)

Sprinkle salt on a small plate. Run a lime wedge around the rim of 2 glasses; dip glasses in salt.

Smash the halved strawberries and chile in a cocktail shaker using the end of a wooden spoon. Fill the shaker ¾ full with ice. Add mezcal, Cointreau, and citrus juices and shake vigorously. Strain the cocktail into small spice-rimmed glasses (filled with ice, if desired). Garnish with whole strawberries.

BAR NOTE: | Espadín is the most common type of mezcal, and it's ideal for mixing into drinks.

Summer Crudités

When it comes to veggie platters, I like a loose, more organic vibe. Start by mounding each type of vegetable on a platter (or downsize to a regular ol' dinner plate to create a full look) in blocks of color like a color wheel. Hold a bunch of carrots (all facing the same direction) and drop them down onto the dish, letting them land naturally. The color blocking gives symmetry, while the free-form mounds feel fresh from the garden. I've learned that when platters look too orderly and immaculate, it can be intimidating for guests to make the approach; a little bit of imperfection is much more inviting.

To assemble the crudités platter in the hot summer months, pack cherry tomatoes, dragon tongue or green beans, cucumbers, baby squash slices, and sweet peppers on top of ice. This will keep the veggies super cool and very crisp.

Julie's Classic Ranch / MAKES ABOUT 2 CUPS

Julie Robles is a wonderful chef and dear friend. She shared this delicious dip when my girls were tots, and it's so good that I basically want to fall headfirst into the bowl and lick it clean. Once the dip is mixed, you can store it in a mason jar in the fridge for about a week. This classic ranch is equally great as a dressing on greens or as a dip for crudités. I think we always associate ranch and kids together, but I have to tell you, this is an equal-opportunity dressing loved by all. Try it at your next dinner party—your people will be stoked.

Tip: It's easy to dry herbs at home by plucking leaves and putting them on a baking sheet in the lowest setting on your oven (180°F to 200°F) until dry, about 1 hour.

1 cup buttermilk

1 cup mayonnaise, such as Best Foods or Hellmann's

1 garlic clove, finely grated

2 teaspoons fresh lemon juice (from ½ lemon)

2 teaspoons dried parsley

1 teaspoon dried dill

¾ teaspoon onion powder

½ teaspoon Diamond Crystal kosher salt

½ teaspoon garlic powder

½ teaspoon freshly cracked pepper

⅛ teaspoon Tabasco hot sauce

Shake all ingredients in a large jar until smooth. Taste for seasoning. *(Can be made 1 week ahead; refrigerate.)*

KITCHEN NOTE: If you want to make it dairy-free, omit the buttermilk and substitute 1 cup raw cashews. Simply soak the nuts overnight in enough cold water to cover by 2 inches. Drain cashews; purée in a blender with remaining ingredients, adding an additional 2 tablespoons of lemon juice to the recipe. To make it vegan, use the soaked cashews and replace regular mayonnaise with vegan mayonnaise.

California Halibut Ceviche

4 SERVINGS

Our local halibut is great for ceviche because it's super fresh and its leanness holds up well to this type of "cooking." The combination of the two acids (lemon and lime) makes the taste of the delicate fish bright and lovely. You can serve it in tortilla baskets (brush warm corn tortillas with oil, season with salt, press into muffin tins, and bake in a hot oven until crisp), or pair the ceviche with guacamole and your favorite brand of tortilla chips.

The ají amarillo pepper is fresh and fruity tasting with medium heat; it's the gold standard of chile to use in Peruvian ceviche. Like most small peppers, it grows very well in SoCal.

CEVICHE
½ pound fresh halibut, bloodline removed, fish
    cut into small dice
½ teaspoon Diamond Crystal kosher salt
1 cup fresh lemon juice (from 5 lemons)
½ cup fresh lime juice (from 4 to 5 limes)
½ cup diced tomatoes (about 1 large tomato)
¼ cup chopped onion (about ¼ onion)
2 tablespoons diced ají amarillo or fresno chiles
    (about 2 chiles)

1 tablespoon minced fresh cilantro stems
½ teaspoon flaky sea salt
10 whole cilantro leaves

PLATING
Guacamole
Tortilla chips, such as Chicas brand

FOR CEVICHE: In a glass bowl, sprinkle the halibut with kosher salt, then cover completely with lemon and lime juice. Cover and refrigerate for at least 1 and up to 3 hours.

Drain the fish, discarding juice. Place fish in a serving bowl. Gently fold in tomatoes, onion, chile, and minced cilantro. Sprinkle with flaky salt and cilantro leaves.

FOR PLATING: Enjoy ceviche with guacamole and chips (or serve in a baked tortilla basket).

BAR NOTE: | Ceviche goes great with crisp white wine like a Sauvignon Blanc or a frosty Mexican beer like Victoria.

Zucchini Feta Fritters with Tahini Yogurt Sauce

4 TO 6 SERVINGS

When you grow zucchini in the summer garden, you can never have enough recipes (see Moroccan Bread & Butter Zucchini Pickles, page 271; Grilled Zucchini with Chile Mint Vinaigrette, page 123; and Fudgy Chocolate Chip Zucchini Loaf Cake with Maple Sour Cream Icing, page 130). Sometimes I get a little overzealous in March with my summer planting, as I am never without lots (and I mean lots) of zucchini. This is a great recipe to plate as a pre-dinner snack for your friends, and it's lovely for a light, summery lunch.

FRITTERS

½ pound zucchini, grated on a box grater (about 2 cups)

½ teaspoon Diamond Crystal kosher salt

2 eggs

¼ cup all-purpose flour

½ teaspoon baking soda

¼ cup cotija or feta cheese, crumbled

3 green onions, finely chopped

¼ cup (packed) chopped fresh Italian parsley

¼ cup (packed) chopped fresh cilantro

¼ cup (packed) chopped fresh mint

½ jalapeño chile, stemmed, seeded, minced

⅛ teaspoon Piment d'Espelette or Aleppo pepper (see Spice Drawer, page 274)

Safflower oil (for frying)

PLATING

Tahini Yogurt Sauce (see recipe, page 265)

Assorted fresh herb sprigs (garnish)

Piment d'Espelette or Aleppo pepper (garnish)

FOR FRITTERS: Toss zucchini with salt in a colander and let stand 15 minutes to release juices. Wrap zucchini in a clean kitchen towel; squeeze dry. Whisk eggs in a large bowl to blend; add flour and baking soda, then cotija, onions, herbs, chile, and ⅛ teaspoon Piment d'Espelette. Mix in zucchini. *(Can be made ahead; cover and chill up to 4 hours.)*

Preheat the oven to 200°F. Line a baking sheet with paper towels. Heat about ¼ cup oil in a heavy large skillet over medium heat. Working in batches, drop batter by mounded tablespoonfuls into oil and cook fritters until golden brown, about 2 minutes per side (add more oil to the skillet as necessary). Keep fritters on the paper towel–lined sheet in a warm oven until ready to serve, or up to 30 minutes.

FOR PLATING: Place fritters on plates. Serve with yogurt sauce, and sprinkle lightly with herb sprigs and Piment d'Espelette.

RAJ TELLS ME... A Provençal-style rosé would be a delight here, as it's a little richer in style than a Sancerre. I like the Domaine La Bastide Blanche Bandol Rosé.

GARDEN NOTE: | To keep your zucchini plant healthy with adequate sunlight and circulation, prune it by removing brown leaves and any large stalks and leaves that intersect.

Mini Squash Blossom Quesadillas

4 SERVINGS

With edible fruit, leaves, and flowers, the zucchini plant is a rock star in the garden. When harvesting the flowers, select male over female flowers. The females are attached to the budding fruit, while the male sits on a long, single stem. Both are needed (so don't pick them all) to produce zucchini. If you harvest baby zucchini early, you can get both the fruit and the flower at once or just snap off the flower from the fruit and let the fruit continue to grow. This is the same preparation for flowers I use to fill omelets.

12 zucchini squash blossoms

1 tablespoon safflower oil

2 garlic cloves, grated

4 zucchini leaves, new growth, cut into strips (optional)

¼ teaspoon flaky sea salt

¼ teaspoon Aleppo pepper (see Spice Drawer, page 274)

2 cups (8 ounces) Oaxacan or mozzarella cheese, coarsely grated, divided

8 4-inch corn tortillas

Avocado & Purple Tomatillo Salsa (see recipe, page 264)

Gently remove the pistil and stamens from the blossoms and wipe clean with a paper towel, keeping flowers intact.

Heat oil in a medium skillet over medium heat. Add garlic and sauté 1 minute or until the garlic perfumes your kitchen. Add zucchini blossoms and leaves (if using), and turn to coat the flowers with all the garlicky goodness. Sprinkle with salt and Aleppo pepper. Set aside.

Heat a heavy large dry skillet over medium-high heat until hot. Sprinkle 2 tablespoons of cheese directly in the skillet and lay 2 tortillas side by side atop the cheese (cheese will turn brown and crisp up, like Frigo). Sprinkle 1 tablespoon more cheese on top of each tortilla and top with a few sautéed zucchini blossoms and leaves, if using. Add a little more cheese to cover and fold over; cook on the other side until the tortilla is crispy and the cheese inside is completely melted. Repeat with remaining cheese, blossoms, and tortillas.

Serve quesadillas with Avocado & Purple Tomatillo Salsa.

RAJ TELLS ME... In Sancerre, wines are made from 100 percent Pinot Noir and are super light and crisp. Try this dish with 2019 Domaine Vacheron Sancerre Rosé.

Rica's Tortilla Soup

4 SERVINGS

Rica Gonzalez is one of my most favorite people in the entire world. She really is like a second mom to me and has taught me so much of what I know about preparing Mexican food. Originally from Durango, she worked for my family for twenty years and now splits her time between Mexico and California. Rica's food is fresh, flavorful, and oh, so tasty; every time she cooks, I get excited. Here is her wonderful and simple tortilla soup.

SOUP

2 cups No-Stir Chicken Stock (see recipe, page 272) or other good-quality chicken stock

4 tomatoes, quartered (about 1½ pounds)

¼ white onion

1 jalapeño chile (seeds optional, stem removed)

1 garlic clove

1 teaspoon Diamond Crystal kosher salt

½ teaspoon freshly ground pepper

TOPPINGS

¾ cup grapeseed or safflower oil

6 small corn tortillas, cut into ½-inch-wide strips

Flaky sea salt

½ avocado, cut into large dice

½ cup cubed Monterey Jack cheese

Chopped fresh cilantro

FOR SOUP: In a blender, purée stock, tomatoes, onion, jalapeño, garlic, salt, and pepper. Bring purée to a simmer in a large saucepan.

FOR TOPPINGS: While the soup is simmering, heat oil in a heavy large skillet over medium-high heat. When the oil begins to ripple, add half of the tortilla strips and fry until golden brown, about 3 minutes. Using tongs, remove tortilla strips from the skillet and drain on paper towels. Repeat frying with remaining tortillas. Sprinkle with salt.

Ladle soup into bowls. Top with fried tortillas, avocado, cheese, and cilantro.

RAJ TELLS ME... I prefer a clean-tasting white wine with this soup, like a Grüner Veltliner from the Wachau region of Austria or a Chardonnay that is made in stainless steel rather than oak.

Avocado Slaw

6 SERVINGS

This slaw has been a consistent hit at my house for years, whether it's for a party for fifty or a regular at-home Taco Tuesday night. You can use whatever fresh radishes and cabbage you have on hand. I use a handheld mandoline to slice the carrots and radishes thinly. You can make it a few hours in advance—I even love it the next day.

1 head napa or savoy cabbage (about 2½ pounds)

3 avocados, halved, chopped on the bias

2 carrots, very thinly sliced into rounds

5 radishes, very thinly sliced

½ cup fresh lime juice (from 4 to 5 large limes)

3 tablespoons (packed) cilantro leaves

1 jalapeño chile, halved, seeded, finely chopped

1 teaspoon Diamond Crystal kosher salt

½ teaspoon freshly ground pepper

Cut the cabbage lengthwise in half and then cut lengthwise in half again for a total of 4 quarters. Cut out the core, then cut the cabbage into thin diagonal strips—a sort of julienne vibe. Toss cabbage in a large bowl with the remaining ingredients. *(Can be made 4 hours ahead; cover and refrigerate.)*

Three-Bean Salad with Cherry Tomatoes, Basil & French Vinaigrette

4 TO 6 SERVINGS

Summer beans fresh from the garden are amazingly sweet and a treat to eat right off the stalk. For this salad, I blanch them quickly in boiling water (no more than 1 minute) and then plunge them straight into a bowl of icy water. This method helps soften the beans so they aren't too fibrous. They'll retain that wonderful raw-from-the-garden flavor without losing any of their terrific crunch and color (the Dragon Tongue beans are particularly at risk of this). I love to pair the fresh beans with giant, creamy, dried Corona or Gigante beans, which I always have on hand, thanks to regular online orders from Rancho Gordo (see Resources, page 289).

After burning countless batches of dried beans on the stovetop, I began cooking them in a covered pot in the oven. With this low-maintenance method (no need to check the water level constantly for evaporation), they turn out perfectly every single time. The Gigantes can take anywhere from 1 hour to 3 hours, depending on the age of the bean, so check on them after an hour. If you can't find Gigante beans, you can substitute large lima beans, Mogette de Vendée, or cannellini beans.

1 cup dried Corona or Gigante beans
½ onion, cut in half
1 dried ancho chile (optional)
2 fresh bay leaves
½ pound green beans, blanched
½ pound Dragon Tongue or Purple Bush beans, blanched

1 cup Sungold cherry tomatoes, cut in half
½ cup pitted Kalamata olives, cut in half
⅓ cup fresh basil leaves, torn
¼ cup chopped fresh Italian parsley
French Vinaigrette (see recipe, page 262)

Preheat the oven to 350°F. Place Corona beans, onion, dried chile (if using), and bay leaves in a small to medium Dutch oven with enough water to cover by 3 inches. Bake until tender, up to 3 hours depending on age of the beans. Discard onion, chile, and bay. Drain and cool.

Toss Corona beans, fresh beans, tomatoes, olives, basil, and parsley in a large bowl with enough vinaigrette to taste. *(Can be made 8 hours ahead. Cover and refrigerate.)*

Tomato & Stone Fruit Salad with Sesame Maple Dressing

4 TO 6 SERVINGS

A mixture of summer's best tomatoes, bright, acidic stone fruit, and sweet maple syrup makes this salad so darn delicious and tangy. The dressing has a multitude of uses—try sopping it up with a crisp baguette. It's also great on raw cucumbers or on grilled veggies like eggplant or zucchini.

DRESSING

2 tablespoons plus 1 teaspoon sherry vinegar

2 tablespoons fresh lemon juice (from 1 lemon)

2 tablespoons pure maple syrup

2 tablespoons toasted sesame oil

1 teaspoon flaky sea salt

SALAD

1 basket cherry tomatoes

4 medium tomatoes

2 large heirloom tomatoes

3 yellow nectarines

3 small plums or pluots

Flaky sea salt and freshly ground pepper

2 tablespoons toasted sesame seeds

Opal or Thai basil leaves

FOR DRESSING: Whisk all ingredients in a small bowl to blend. *(Can be made 1 day ahead. Cover and let stand at room temperature.)*

FOR SALAD: Cut small tomatoes in half and large tomatoes and stone fruit into quarters and arrange on a platter. Season with salt and pepper. When you are ready to serve, drizzle dressing over the salad and sprinkle with sesame seeds and basil.

GARDEN NOTE: | When selecting tomatoes to plant in your garden, keep in mind that their color greatly affects the taste. Red or pink tomatoes have more sugar than acid. Orange and yellow tomatoes are less acidic than other varieties and also milder in flavor. Black and purples have a complexity of umami, with earthiness and a balanced flavor.

Melon with Lemon Verbena & Serrano Ham

4 TO 6 SERVINGS

This is an easy way to start a meal that celebrates summer. Cool, sweet summer melon with salty ham and fragrant verbena leaves is fresh and delicious, with no pots and pans required. Ambrosia melon looks similar to a cantaloupe, but it's sweeter and very floral. We grow it on trellises in full sun.

1 Ambrosia or cantaloupe melon, peeled, cut into 2-inch wedges

5 fresh lemon verbena leaves, torn

8 slices Serrano ham or prosciutto di Parma

Extra-virgin olive oil

¼ teaspoon flaky sea salt

½ teaspoon freshly cracked pepper

Fresh lemon verbena sprigs (garnish)

Cut melon in half; scoop out seeds. Cut each half into 4 wedges. Using a sharp knife, cut down the length of each melon wedge between the flesh and skin, leaving it attached at one end. Sprinkle melon with torn lemon verbena leaves. Refrigerate until ready to assemble, at least 1 hour and up to 4 hours.

Place melon on a platter, discarding the torn verbena. Fold ham slices crosswise in half and coil loosely. Arrange ham alongside melon. Drizzle melon with oil. Sprinkle with salt and pepper. Garnish with lemon verbena sprigs.

Rigatoni with Heirloom Tomato Sauce

4 TO 6 SERVINGS

One of my main motivations for planting tomatoes in multiples is to have beautiful, tasty ingredients at my fingertips. On those warm, lazy nights when I can't decide what to make (and truthfully, I probably forgot to go to the store), I go out back, pluck a few tomatoes, grab some dried pasta, and a celebratory summer meal is born. I like to use rigatoni here because the ridges of the tube fully embrace the garden tomato flavor.

1 pound dried rigatoni

Heirloom Tomato Sauce (see recipe, page 267)

Freshly ground pepper

2 water-packed buffalo mozzarella balls, drained, cut into large dice

Extra-virgin olive oil

Fresh basil leaves, torn

½ cup coarsely shredded parmesan

Cook pasta in a large pot of boiling salted water until just tender but still firm to bite, stirring occasionally, about 12 minutes. Remove ½ cup pasta cooking liquid and reserve. Drain pasta.

Bring tomato sauce to simmer in a large pot. Add the pasta and about ¼ cup reserved pasta water and toss to mix well, adding more water if dry. Season with pepper; portion the pasta into 4 to 6 dishes. Top with mozzarella, a drizzle of olive oil, then sprinkle with basil and parmesan.

RAJ TELLS ME... This is recommended with a light-bodied Sangiovese, such as a Montevertine from Tuscany or a Stolpman "Love You Bunches" from Santa Barbara County.

Eggplant Gratin with Mozzarella, Heirloom Tomato Sauce & Basil

6 SERVINGS

I grow a wide variety of heirloom eggplants; my favorites are purple Japanese, Listada de Gandia, Rosa Bianca, Edirne purple striped, and Rosita. I usually plant a few of each, and the garden looks like a jewel box of white, purple, and pink, with speckles and stripes—it's fun to grow, harvest, and eat something so gorgeous. Eggplants need full sun and, like their nightshade cousin the tomato, have a long growing season that sets fruit deep into the fall.

This recipe is a family favorite that's simple to put together. The traditional American eggplant acts like a sponge when it meets oil, but the heirloom Japanese and Italian varieties I grow are less spongy, less bitter, and have thinner skins—which means there's no need to salt, bread, just slice and roast in a hot oven, layer with tomato sauce and cheese, and you're on your way to a lighter meal.

6 medium heirloom eggplants (unpeeled), sliced lengthwise into ⅓-inch-thick slices (about 1½ pounds)

Extra-virgin olive oil (for brushing), plus 1 tablespoon

Diamond Crystal kosher salt and freshly ground pepper

2½ cups Heirloom Tomato Sauce (see recipe, page 267)

3 tablespoons chopped fresh basil

2 cups grated mozzarella cheese

¾ cup freshly grated parmesan

2 tablespoons panko breadcrumbs

Preheat the oven to 450°F. Place eggplant in a single layer on 1 to 2 baking sheets. Brush both sides of eggplant generously with oil and season with salt and pepper. Bake until tender and golden brown, about 16 to 18 minutes. Cool. (*Eggplant can be made 1 day ahead. Cover and chill.*)

Preheat the oven to 400°F. Brush 12 x 8-inch oval gratin baking dish or medium casserole with oil. Spread 2 tablespoons sauce over the bottom, then top with ⅓ of the eggplant. Spoon ¾ cup tomato sauce over eggplant.

Sprinkle with half of basil, half of mozzarella and half of parmesan. Top with half of the remaining eggplant. Spoon ¾ tomato sauce over the eggplant and sprinkle with remaining basil, mozzarella, and parmesan. Arrange remaining eggplant over the cheese and top with remaining sauce.

Mix breadcrumbs and 1 tablespoon oil in a small bowl. Sprinkle the breadcrumbs over the sauce. Bake until the casserole bubbles at the sides and is heated through, about 35 minutes.

RAJ TELLS ME... This Mediterranean dish just calls out for a slightly chilled Barbera, like the Sottimano from Piedmont or the Idlewild from Mendocino.

Grilled Salmon in Fig Leaves with Nectarine Relish

6 SERVINGS

In California, salmon season runs from April to August, just when the leaves from our fig trees happen to be big and tender. When picking fig leaves, select ones that are growing in multiples. They protect the fruit from the sun, so watch for exposing the figs.

Grilling fish like this is a great technique because 1) the fish doesn't stick to the grill, 2) it tastes amazing (the fig leaves impart a coconut-like flavor), and 3) it uses what's growing in the garden. The tangy yellow nectarine relish is equally as good on fish as it is on simply grilled poultry.

NECTARINE RELISH

1 cup diced yellow nectarine or peach (about 1 large)

¼ cup chopped green onions (white and pale green parts only; about 2 onions)

¼ cup extra-virgin olive oil

2 tablespoons (packed) chopped fresh basil

2 tablespoons chopped Preserved Meyer Lemons (see recipe, page 270)

2 tablespoons white balsamic vinegar

1 fresno chile or small jalapeño, stemmed, seeded, and diced

½ teaspoon Aleppo pepper (see Spice Drawer, page 274)

FISH

6 4-ounce salmon or halibut fillets, pin bones and skin removed

Extra-virgin olive oil

Flaky sea salt and freshly ground white pepper

6 large fresh fig leaves, rinsed, stems removed

FOR RELISH: Mix all ingredients in a small bowl. *(Can be made 6 hours ahead. Cover and refrigerate.)*

FOR FISH: Brush both sides of the fish with olive oil and season with salt and pepper. Place 1 fig leaf, shiny side down, on a rimmed baking sheet; top with 1 fish fillet. Wrap the leaf around the fish like you would a present. Turn the fish over so its weight secures the leaves in place. Repeat, wrapping remaining leaves and fillets. *(Can be made 4 to 6 hours ahead. Cover fish; place a small bag of ice over the fish to keep extra cold and refrigerate.)*

Preheat the oven to 400°F or fire up the barbecue. Bake fish until just cooked through, 10 to 12 minutes, depending on the thickness of the fish (general rule of thumb is 5 minutes per inch of thickness). Or cook fish on the grill using indirect heat with the lid closed (as the fish cooks, the fig leaves will form a secure wrapping around the fish).

Place the fish packages in their leaves on a platter or plate them individually. Remove the leaves. Serve with relish.

RAJ TELLS ME... Since the dish has some spice from the relish, a light and fresh gamay would be a delicious choice—perhaps the Dutraive Fleurie from Beaujolais or Evening Land's "Seven Springs" from the Willamette Valley.

Carnitas Tacos with Homemade Tortillas

10 TO 12 SERVINGS

Pork shoulder cooked low and slow makes these simple tacos so delicious and succulent. Try your hand at making the tortillas from scratch, as they enhance the dish, or seek out quality tortillas from your favorite Mexican market or taco stand. Serve these tacos with Avocado Slaw (page 103), Roasted Garden Salsa (page 263), and Green Garden Rice (page 120).

4- to 5-pound pork shoulder or butt roast
½ cup brown sugar
½ cup Diamond Crystal kosher salt
Freshly ground pepper

½ white onion, chopped, soaked in water for 20 minutes and drained
½ cup whole cilantro leaves
Double recipe Homemade Tortillas (see recipe, page 268), warm

Place pork in a large casserole dish. Mix sugar and salt and rub all over pork. Cover and refrigerate for at least 6 hours or overnight.

Preheat the oven to 300°F. Rinse off the sugar and salt from the pork; dry the meat very well with kitchen towels. Place the pork in a large roasting pan and sprinkle liberally with pepper. Roast pork until tender and pulls apart easily with a fork, occasionally spooning the fat over the roast to baste, about 6 hours.

Shred the pork by moving two forks across pork in opposite directions. Mound meat on a heat-proof platter. Taste and season to your liking with salt and pepper; keep warm in a low 200°F oven.

Mix onion and cilantro together. Warm the tortillas in a cast-iron skillet or comal and keep warm in a cloth-lined basket. Spoon the pork into warm tortillas and sprinkle with onion and cilantro.

Tip: To heat the tortillas in advance, warm them on the comal or skillet, wrap them in a dish towel, and immediately nestle them in a small cooler. The tortillas will stay warm for at least an hour.

RAJ TELLS ME... Cross the border for more than tacos—look for Bichi Mission "Listan" from Tecate, Mexico; if you can't find it, consider the Monte Rio Mission from Lodi, California.

Orange-Marinated Tri-Tip with Chimichurri & Padrón Peppers

6 SERVINGS

Nothing could get more California than citrus-marinated tri-tip. This triangular cut of meat from the bottom sirloin is a Central Coast specialty, and it's on regular rotation at our house during barbecue season—especially when we have guests from Europe or the East Coast. For the best flavor, seek out a well-marbled roast.

Padrón peppers are similar to shishitos but with more flavor and a tad more heat. Both grow in a bush-like fashion and often need a bamboo support to hold up the mass of leaves and yield. As it happens in the summer when you have a garden and travel plans, some things get ignored and become overripe. This is how I discovered how delicious padrón and shishito peppers are when you leave them to get red. They become sweeter as they mature—I wish that were the case for all of us. On their own, they can be served as a simple summer appetizer.

BEEF
2 pounds trimmed well-marbled tri-tip
½ cup fresh orange juice (from 2 oranges)
¼ cup soy sauce
¼ cup olive oil
½ onion, sliced
4 garlic cloves, smashed
½ teaspoon dried red chile flakes

PADRÓN PEPPERS
2 tablespoons grapeseed oil
20 padrón or shishito peppers
½ teaspoon flaky sea salt
½ teaspoon sumac (see Spice Drawer, page 274)
Orange wedges (optional)
Chimichurri Sauce (see recipe, page 264)

FOR BEEF: Combine tri-tip, orange juice, soy sauce, oil, onion, garlic, and chile flakes in a large resealable plastic bag. Refrigerate for at least 4 hours or overnight, turning the bag halfway through the marinating process.

Prepare the grill for direct and indirect cooking. Pat beef dry with paper towels and season with salt and pepper. Over direct heat, sear the fat side of the beef for 2 to 3 minutes to create some caramelization. Turn the beef over and place on indirect heat (you are basically using your grill like an oven at this point). Cover and continue to cook until an instant-read thermometer inserted into the center of the beef registers 120°F for rare or 130°F for medium rare, turning occasionally, 20 to 25 minutes. Let beef rest for 15 minutes.

FOR PEPPERS: While beef rests, prepare peppers. In a large skillet, heat oil on medium-high heat until hot. Add the peppers and sauté until they begin to blister, about 3 to 5 minutes. Add sea salt and sumac and toss to coat.

Thinly slice the meat perpendicular to the grain. Surround with peppers, oranges (if desired), and sauce.

RAJ TELLS ME… A light, fresh cab franc from Chinon is excellent with this dish; we like Catherine & Pierre Breton Chinon "Beaumont" from the Loire and Habit Cabernet Franc from Santa Ynez Valley.

Creamed White Corn Gratin

4 TO 6 SERVINGS

Don't skip cooking the corn first, it helps release the amazing juices from the cob.

6 fresh corn cobs, shucked
4 tablespoons butter, divided
¼ cup finely chopped onion
1 tablespoon all-purpose flour
1 cup whole milk
¼ cup crème fraîche
1 teaspoon Diamond Crystal kosher salt
½ teaspoon Aleppo pepper (see Spice Drawer, page 274)
½ teaspoon freshly ground pepper
½ cup freshly grated parmesan

Cook corn in a pot of boiling water for 5 minutes. Drain; cut kernels off cob. Place corn in a bowl. Working over the bowl, run the flat side of a large knife against the cob to extract any juices.

Melt 3 tablespoons butter in a large skillet over medium-high heat. Add onion and sauté until light golden brown, about 5 minutes. Add the flour and stir until flour is cooked, 1 to 2 minutes. Whisk in milk and crème fraîche and bring to a boil. Mix in corn, salt, and both peppers.

Preheat broiler, positioning rack 5 to 6 inches from the heat source. Grease a shallow 12 x 8–inch oval gratin baking dish or medium casserole with remaining 1 tablespoon butter; add the corn mixture. Sprinkle with cheese. Broil gratin until bubbly and golden brown, about 10 minutes. Serve warm.

Green Garden Rice

4 SERVINGS

1 cup water
2 medium tomatillos, husks removed
½ cup (packed) arugula
½ cup (packed) cilantro leaves and stems
¼ yellow or white onion
2 garlic cloves
1 teaspoon Diamond Crystal kosher salt
1 tablespoon extra-virgin olive oil
1 cup jasmine rice

In a blender, purée water, tomatillos, arugula, cilantro, onion, garlic, and salt.

Heat oil in a medium sauté pan fitted with a lid over medium heat. Add rice and sauté until it smells nutty and is golden in color, about 3 minutes. Mix in purée and bring to a boil. Reduce heat to low. Cover and simmer until rice is tender and liquid is almost absorbed, 12 to 15 minutes. Remove from heat. Cover and let stand 5 minutes. Fluff rice with a fork and serve.

Grilled Zucchini with Chile Mint Vinaigrette

4 TO 6 SERVINGS

This recipe is equally delicious with whatever squash you have on hand. I like planting a variety, my favorites being the grey zucchini and romanesco squash because they have an earthy flavor and creamier texture when cooked. Fresno peppers are easy to grow and more flavorful than jalapeños. They don't need a lot of space to grow, just full sun and a terracotta pot and you're in business.

¼ cup extra-virgin olive oil, plus more for brushing

1 green onion (white and light green parts only), thinly sliced

1 fresno chile or ½ jalapeño, very thinly sliced

1 small garlic clove, very thinly sliced

1 tablespoon red wine vinegar

1 tablespoon fresh lemon juice (from ½ lemon)

1 tablespoon finely chopped fresh mint

1 teaspoon grated lemon peel (from 1 lemon)

½ teaspoon Diamond Crystal kosher salt

¼ teaspoon freshly ground pepper

4 zucchini or yellow squash

Flaky sea salt

½ cup cherry tomatoes, cut in half

Fresh mint leaves (garnish)

Prepare barbecue grill (medium-high heat). Whisk together oil, onion, chile, garlic, red wine vinegar, lemon juice, mint, lemon peel, salt, and pepper in a small bowl. Set vinaigrette aside.

Cut the zucchini lengthwise into ¼-inch-thick slices (keep some of the stem on so it looks pretty). Brush with oil and sprinkle with sea salt. Grill zucchini until lightly charred, turning occasionally, 5 to 7 minutes. Arrange zucchini on a platter; drizzle with half of the vinaigrette, adding more if desired. Sprinkle with tomatoes and mint leaves.

Heirloom Eggplant with Cilantro Chutney

4 TO 6 SERVINGS

This tasty dish uses our summer harvest baskets of eggplant. It even makes a wonderful main course for a light vegetarian dinner on a hot summer night, served with a chilled rosé.

SAUCE

2 cups (packed) cilantro leaves and stems
¼ cup extra-virgin olive oil
¼ cup water
1 2-inch piece fresh ginger, peeled
2 garlic cloves
1 small jalapeño, stemmed, cut in half
1 teaspoon grated lemon zest (from 1 lemon)

EGGPLANT

¼ cup extra-virgin olive oil or ghee
2 medium heirloom eggplants, cut into large 2-inch dice
2 teaspoons Diamond Crystal kosher salt
¼ cup Greek yogurt
¼ cup Crispy Chickpeas with Ras el Hanout (see recipe at right)
Cilantro sprigs (garnish)

FOR SAUCE: Purée all ingredients in a food processor. *(Cilantro sauce can be made 4 hours ahead. Cover and refrigerate.)*

FOR EGGPLANT: In a very large skillet or wok, heat the oil over medium-high heat until hot. Once the oil starts to dance around the pan, add eggplant, seasoning with salt as you do so, and sauté until tender, about 15 minutes. Transfer to a platter. Top eggplant with yogurt and chickpeas and garnish with cilantro sprigs. Serve with cilantro sauce.

Crispy Chickpeas with Ras el Hanout

MAKES ABOUT 1 CUP

These crispy chickpeas are the perfect garnish for the Eggplant with Cilantro Chutney. They add a great crunch and a yummy pop of flavor. We like them so much we often serve them solo in a small bowl as a bar snack.

1 15-ounce can garbanzo beans (chickpeas), rinsed, drained, patted dry
1 tablespoon extra-virgin olive oil
1 teaspoon ras el hanout (see Spice Drawer, page 274)
Diamond Crystal kosher salt

Preheat the oven to 425°F. Toss the garbanzo beans with olive oil and ras el hanout on a heavy large rimmed baking sheet. Sprinkle with salt. Roast chickpeas until lightly browned and fragrant, shaking pan once or twice, about 12 minutes. Serve warm or at room temperature. *(Can be made 2 hours ahead. Let stand at room temperature.)*

Roasted Stone Fruit with Amarena Cherry Syrup

6 SERVINGS

Candied sour cherries from Italy are deep, dark, and complexly flavored—one of my favorite cocktail garnishes. When I've dropped that last cherry into an icy Black Manhattan (page 206), I'm left with a jar of delicious syrup—the perfect sweetener for roasted plums, peaches, nectarines, pluots, and cherries.

2 tablespoons (¼ stick) butter
2 pounds mixed stone fruit (such as plums, peaches, nectarines, and pluots, pitted and sliced; plus pitted cherries)

¼ cup Amarena cherry syrup (see Bar Extras, page 287)
Vanilla ice cream
Walnut Lavender Shortbread (see recipe, page 127)

Preheat the oven to 450°F. Heat the butter in a heavy large rimmed baking sheet in the oven until just melted. Add the fruit and drizzle evenly with the syrup. Roast until the fruit is tender, stirring gently once or twice, about 20 minutes. Serve warm with your favorite vanilla ice cream and shortbread.

Walnut Lavender Shortbread

8 SERVINGS

Lavandula angustifolia, or English lavender, is my all-time-favorite perennial border. Not only is it fragrant and whimsical, but it's drought tolerant and you can harvest it for baking cookies like this recipe below. Use the petals fresh or dried, but no matter how you use it, know that a little goes a long way. To harvest and dry, simply snip the stem of the plant where the leaves end and then hang upside down or lay flat in a cool, dry place. When you're ready to cook with the lavender, rub the buds together with your thumb and forefinger, and the petals will separate.

This cookie is a very pretty cookie to gift. After it cools, place the entire round on a cardboard cake round and wrap the whole thing in cellophane. Tie it with a bow, tucking in a few dried lavender stems.

Melted butter (for brushing)

2 cups all-purpose flour

1 teaspoon flaky sea salt

1 cup (2 sticks) unsalted butter, room temperature

¼ cup sugar

1 teaspoon freshly picked lavender petals or dried culinary lavender

1 teaspoon vanilla extract

1 cup walnuts, toasted, finely chopped

Powdered sugar

Preheat the oven to 325°F. Generously brush a 9-inch-diameter tart pan with a removable bottom with butter. Whisk flour and salt to blend in a medium bowl. In a large bowl and using an electric mixer, beat 1 cup butter, ¼ cup sugar, lavender, and vanilla until light and fluffy. Mix in flour mixture and walnuts. Press the dough evenly into the prepared pan. Using fork tines, mark the round into 8 wedges.

Bake until the shortbread is golden brown, about 20 minutes. Transfer the pan to a rack and, using the marks as guides, cut warm shortbread into wedges. Cool completely. Sprinkle with powdered sugar. *(Can be made up to 3 days ahead. Store in an airtight container at room temperature.)*

Lemon Chiffon Cupcakes with Rose Petals

MAKES ABOUT 16 CUPCAKES

The rose garden in our yard is a labor of love. I have had as many failures as successes. Over the years I have gotten more picky about what I plant because, let's face it, roses are expensive and, honestly, they can be fickle. But when they are good, they are sooo so worth any trial or tribulation! I'm a sucker for David Austin roses in particular, an English breed known for its amazing aromas and gloriously plentiful petals reminiscent of cabbages. When choosing roses, I look for disease-resistant varieties, ones that don't shatter easily (this is harder than you think and especially hard when growing Austins), ones known to grow well in my climate, and ones that look good with the colors in our home. Super light and super summery.

CUPCAKES
1 cup plus 2 tablespoons cake flour

¾ cup sugar, divided

1½ teaspoons baking powder

1 teaspoon Diamond Crystal kosher salt

¼ cup safflower or grapeseed oil

3 tablespoons water

3 tablespoons fresh lemon juice (from 2 lemons)

3 large egg yolks

1 tablespoon grated lemon zest (from 2 lemons)

1 large egg white

¼ teaspoon cream of tartar

GLAZE
1½ cups powdered sugar

1 tablespoon fresh lemon juice (from ½ lemon)

1½ teaspoons grated lemon zest (from 1 lemon)

Candied Citrus Slices (made with lemon; see recipe, page 273)

Unsprayed rose petals (optional)

FOR CUPCAKES: Position rack in the center of the oven and preheat to 350°F. Line cupcake molds with paper cupcake liners. Mix flour, ½ cup sugar, baking powder, and salt in a medium bowl. Whisk the oil, water, lemon juice, egg yolks, and lemon zest in a large bowl to blend, then whisk in dry ingredients.

Using an electric mixer, beat the egg white in a medium metal bowl until foamy. Add the cream of tartar and beat until soft peaks form. Gradually beat in the remaining ¼ cup sugar and continue beating until stiff, shiny peaks form. Using a rubber spatula, stir about ⅓ of the egg white into the batter mixture to lighten it. Gently fold in the remaining egg white.

Carefully spoon the batter into the cupcake liners, dividing evenly; a large ice cream scoop works very well here. Bake the cupcakes until a tester inserted into the center comes out clean, just firm to the touch, about 15 minutes. Cool cupcakes completely on racks.

FOR GLAZE: Whisk sugar, lemon juice, and lemon zest to blend in a medium bowl. Thin by adding water by ½ teaspoonfuls, if necessary. Spoon the glaze over the cupcakes and let stand until set. Garnish with candied lemon and rose petals, if desired. (*Can be made 1 day ahead. Store in an airtight container at room temperature.*)

Fudgy Chocolate Chip Zucchini Loaf Cake with Maple Sour Cream Icing

8 SERVINGS

This is our teenagers' favorite way to use up the zucchini growing out back. For about a blink of an eye, we had a Southern grocery store chain in Santa Barbara, and I got hooked on White Lily self-rising flour. It's a staple in my pantry because it's light, lovely, and easy to use.

CAKE
3 cups grated zucchini (about 2 medium zucchini)
1½ teaspoons Diamond Crystal kosher salt, divided
1½ cups self-rising flour, such as White Lily or King Arthur
1 cup sugar
⅓ cup Dutch process cocoa powder
½ cup (1 stick) butter, melted
2 eggs

⅓ cup buttermilk
2 teaspoons vanilla extract
1 cup semisweet chocolate chips (6 ounces)

ICING
1¼ cups powdered sugar
¼ cup sour cream
1 tablespoon pure maple syrup
½ teaspoon flaky sea salt
Zucchini leaves (for garnish; optional)

FOR CAKE: Preheat the oven to 350°F. Butter a 9 x 5-inch loaf pan. Toss zucchini with 1 teaspoon salt in a bowl and let sit for 30 minutes. Drain zucchini and squeeze dry in a clean kitchen towel. In a large mixing bowl, whisk flour, sugar, cocoa, and remaining ½ teaspoon salt to blend. In another bowl, whisk melted butter, eggs, buttermilk, and vanilla to blend. Stir the wet ingredients into the dry until smooth. Mix in the zucchini and the chocolate chips.

Transfer batter to the prepared pan and bake until a toothpick inserted into the center comes out clean, 40 to 45 minutes. Cool the cake in the pan on a rack for 15 minutes. Turn the cake out and cool completely.

FOR ICING: Whisk sugar, sour cream, syrup, and salt in a bowl until smooth. Spoon icing over cake. Garnish with zucchini leaves, if desired. They are edible, you know.

Strawberry Coconut Sorbet
with White Chocolate–Dipped Coconut Cones

6 SERVINGS

SORBET

2 pints strawberries (about 2 pounds), hulled,
    halved

½ cup canned light coconut milk

¼ cup sugar

2 tablespoons fresh lime juice (from 1 to 2 limes)

DIPPED CONES

¾ cup chopped white chocolate (4 ounces)

6 sugar cones

½ cup unsweetened finely shredded coconut

FOR SORBET: Purée strawberries, coconut milk, sugar, and lime juice in a blender. Process in an ice cream maker according to manufacturer's instructions. Transfer sorbet to a container; freeze until firm enough to scoop. *(Can be made 1 day ahead; keep frozen.)*

FOR CONES: Melt the chocolate in a small bowl set over a saucepan of simmering water, stirring until smooth. Remove from heat. Working with 1 cone at a time, dip the top of the cone into the melted chocolate, tilting pan if necessary to cover 1 inch of cone; let the excess drip off. Then roll the coated portion of the cone into coconut; place upright in juice glasses until the chocolate sets. *(Can be made 6 hours ahead. Let stand at room temperature.)*

Scoop sorbet onto cones. Sprinkle with more coconut, if desired. Enjoy!

Belgian Beer Waffles with Beet Sugar & Summer Jams

MAKES 12 TO 14 WAFFLES

Plug in the iron and mix up the batter. These waffles are easy and delicious, and there is no proofing time required. Patience and planning are not my best skill sets; so on those mornings when I'm short on time and have starving teens staring me down, this is my go-to recipe. Don't be nervous about using the beer and feeding it to the kids. The alcohol dissipates during the cooking process (I promise you won't have belching babies at breakfast calling you Norm!). Track down beet sugar on Amazon.

In the summer, I often make jam with any of our remaining apricot and berry harvests (see Pantry, page 262). Not huge batches for putting up (which needs a lot of prep and planning), but rather a pint or two that I can make quickly and store in the refrigerator.

WAFFLES

1¼ cups Sonora wheat flour or white whole wheat flour

1¼ cups all-purpose flour

2 teaspoons baking soda

2 teaspoons Diamond Crystal kosher salt

2 eggs, whisked

½ cup (1 stick) butter, melted, plus more for cooking

1 tablespoon lemon juice (from 1 lemon)

1 teaspoon vanilla extract

1 8-ounce bottle pilsner beer, such as Stella Artois, divided

½ cup Belgian pearled beet sugar

PLATING

Apricot Jam with Lemon Verbena (see recipe, page 269)

Blackberry & Mulberry Jam (see recipe, page 270)

Butter, room temperature

Powdered sugar

FOR WAFFLES: In a large bowl, whisk together both flours, baking soda, and salt. Make a well in the flour and add eggs, ½ cup melted butter, lemon juice, vanilla, and half of the beer and whisk to incorporate completely. Whisk in the remaining beer. *(Batter can be made 1 day ahead. Cover and refrigerate.)*

The last step is mixing in the pearled sugar and should be done right before you make the waffles. When ready to cook, heat up your waffle iron and stir pearled sugar into the batter. Brush iron with melted butter, ladle in ¼ cup of batter, and cook until golden, about 2 to 3 minutes.

FOR PLATING: Serve waffles with jams or plain with butter and a sprinkling of powdered sugar.

fall

Fall:
Chaos, Cool & Thankfulness

IT IS AROUND THE FAMILY AND THE HOME THAT ALL THE GREATEST VIRTUES ARE CREATED,
STRENGTHENED, AND MAINTAINED.
— WINSTON CHURCHILL

For families with children, after the lovely lull of summer comes to a close, fall can feel like you've been drop-kicked into a whirling dervish. Suddenly days are filled with carpool, work meetings, volunteer obligations, and sports matches, all sandwiched between Halloween, Thanksgiving, houseguests, and maybe a few birthdays thrown into the mix. Damn, it's chaotic, but levity and home-cooked meals need not disappear. I lean on dishes like Fall Tomato Salad with Dandelion Pesto & Honey (page 164) and Hope Ranch Mussels with Chorizo & Fennel (page 167); these recipes are delicious and nutritious but can be made ahead or thrown together quickly. Even with all the bustle and hustle, fall is my absolute favorite time of year, a season rich with family, feasting, and celebration. And those Indian summer nights are what dreams are made of.

The garden needs extra TLC in the fall, after summer's nightshades have sucked the nitrogen right out of your soil. A nice blanket of compost and an additional dose of organic fertilizer will help rejuvenate the depletion. Summer squash like delicata and kabocha are sweetened by their time tucked away in storage and finally at their peak for dips (page 149) and soup (page 156) in the fall.

With brassicas growing large, an abundance of bitter fall greens, and tomatoes and eggplants still finishing their summer shift, garden space is tight, so I'm super selective about what I plant. Out with the ordinary broccoli and cauliflower—they take up a huge amount of precious space, and I can buy good organic varieties at many markets—and in with the harder-to-find chartreuse romanesco and purple sprouting broccoli. In fall, my dates, pomegranates, and pineapple guavas are also ready to harvest.

This chapter includes my tried-and-true Thanksgiving recipes, including Roasted Heritage Turkey with Thyme & Black Pepper Gravy (page 171), Ciabatta Stuffing with Sausage & Sage (page 184), and Mincemeat Pie (page 189). The best part about cooking the Thanksgiving meal is that if you screw something up, you'll get the chance to do it all over again next year with the exact same menu. Just take a deep breath, pour a glass of wine, and enjoy—you're with your nearest and dearest. Oh, and don't underestimate the power of a kick-ass gravy.

People think of Thanksgiving as one meal, but often it means having overnight houseguests, so you're really planning many meals. In anticipation of the week, I have a few trusted recipes that I make in advance and put out for self-service, like the Quiche with Swiss Chard & Leek (page 174), which works for breakfast, lunch, or dinner. Breakfast is prepared way in advance with Honey & Maple Syrup Granola (page 272) and a pretty fruit platter, both of which can sit out buffet-style for late-sleeping teens or early-rising in-laws.

Most importantly, in this season of feasting and fun, be sure not to overlook the obvious—step out of the kitchen for a few minutes of quiet to reflect on all the things you're thankful for. Then go give your people a hug and feed them.

WHAT TO PLANT NOW

If you grow these foods, you'll be able to cook from your garden in the next chapter. I get busy around the autumnal equinox (about September 20th) and start planting for winter. For planting tips, see page 279.

CASTELFRANCO RADICCHIO	PURPLE CAULIFLOWER	ROMANESCO BROCCOLI & PURPLE SPROUTING BROCCOLI	FLORENCE FENNEL
SAVOY CABBAGE & BOK CHOY	CARROTS: ROYAL CHANTENAY & PARISIENNE	TALL UTAH CELERY OR GIANT RED CELERY	HARRIS MODEL PARSNIPS
JAPANESE SWEET POTATOES	SHOGOIN TURNIPS	FRENCH BREAKFAST & WATERMELON RADISHES	MÂCHE OR WATERCRESS
EARLY WONDER BEETS & GOLDEN BEETS	LEEKS	SWISS CHARD	CHERVIL, DILL, MINT, TARRAGON

Fall Recipes

Fall Drinks

1. TAMARIND MARGARITAS (PAGE 144)   2. PETITE DIRTY MARTINI (PAGE 144)
3. CASA RICE MARGARITAS (PAGE 145)   4. LEMON ROSE MARTINIS (PAGE 145)

1.

2.

3.

4.

Tamarind Margaritas

MAKES 2 BIG COCKTAILS

I'm obsessed with Mexican tamarind candy covered in chile powder, and this cocktail has a similar tang, sweetness, and spice. While we garnish the drink with whole peeled tamarind pods for nibbling, we mix the drink with Aunt Patty's Tamarind Paste; it's organic, non-GMO, and beautifully strained.

1 lime wedge
1 tablespoon Spiced Rimming Salt (see recipe, page 271)
4 ounces (½ cup) fresh orange juice (from 2 oranges)
4 ounces (¼ cup) tequila blanco, like Cimarron or Herradura
1 ounce (2 tablespoons) fresh lime juice (from 1 to 2 limes)
1 ounce (2 tablespoons) Cointreau
2 tablespoons tamarind paste
2 lime wheels (garnish)
2 tamarind pods (optional garnish)

Run a lime wedge around the rim of 2 short glasses and dip glasses in Spiced Rimming Salt on a small plate. Fill a large cocktail shaker ¾ full with ice. Add orange juice, tequila, lime juice, Cointreau, and tamarind paste; shake vigorously.

Fill spice-rimmed glasses with ice. Strain contents of shaker into glasses. Garnish with lime wheels and tamarind pods, if desired.

Petite Dirty Martinis

MAKES 2 COCKTAILS

I love the idea of a martini, but often its size is too much of…uh, a "commitment"…before I start dinner. If I drink a whole one, I'll be better off ordering pizza delivery than tackling a meal on a hot stove. To solve this dilemma, I have a little collection of "Nick and Nora" coupe stemware. About a third of the size of a normal martini glass, these little babies are the perfect size for me to deliver dinner myself, and they stay cool as I sip.

Try to find Castelvetrano green olives in a simple salt brine, with pits and all—they taste great and hold up better than a typical martini olive, and the brine makes the best dirty martinis.

4 green Castelvetrano olives with pits
2 ounces (¼ cup) Hendrick's, Gin Mare, or The Botanist gin
2 ounces (¼ cup) Fords Gin or Old Raj
1 ounce (2 tablespoons) olive juice

Fill 2 petite martini glasses with ice to chill. Skewer 2 olives on each toothpick (yes, you can bypass the pit) and place one in each glass. Fill a cocktail pitcher halfway with ice. Add gin and olive juice, and stir for about 20 seconds. Remove the ice in the glassware and strain the contents of the pitcher into the glasses. Garnish with olives.

BAR NOTE: The combination of the two gin styles (see Bar Tips & Tools, page 283) makes this martini super special. Feel free to experiment with your favorite brands or even combine a gin and a vodka.

Casa Rice Margaritas

MAKES 2 COCKTAILS

Just three main ingredients, none of which is agave or simple syrup, make up this tasty, classic margarita. Our Bearss lime trees are the first to hit the citrus scene in fall, producing plump and juicy fruit. If you're using store-bought limes, roll them on the counter with the palm of your hand until warm. This will help release the juices and give you a little hand massage while you're at it.

1 lime wedge
Flaky sea salt (optional)
4 ounces (½ cup) tequila reposado, such as Tequila Ocho or Espolòn Reposado
2 ounces (¼ cup) triple sec, like Cointreau or dry Curaçao
2 ounces (¼ cup) fresh lime juice (from 2 to 3 limes)
Lime wheels (garnish)

Run a lime wedge around the rim of 2 short glasses and dip in sea salt, if desired. Fill glasses with ice. Fill a cocktail shaker ¾ full with ice; add tequila, triple sec, and lime juice, and shake like the dickens. Strain into glasses. Garnish with lime wheels.

Lemon Rose Martinis

MAKES 2 COCKTAILS

Make sure you use unwaxed lemons, fresh roses (unsprayed, please and thank you), and top-shelf booze for this cocktail. I use David Austin pink Boscobel roses, which are remarkably fragrant and stacked with dark pink petals. Layering the lemon and rose with cardamom adds aromatic notes that marry well with bitters and are perfect for fall. The leftover lemon rose syrup is great mixed with sparkling water for a nonalcoholic beverage.

2 Meyer lemons
½ cup sugar
Rose petals from 2 large roses (6 petals reserved for garnish)
2 whole cardamom pods, cracked
4 ounces (½ cup) vodka or London dry gin
Old-fashioned bitters
Pink peppercorns (optional, for garnish)

On the largest side of a box grater, grate 2 lemons, skin and all, in a large bowl. Add the sugar, rose petals, and cardamon, and stir to combine. Cover and let stand 3 to 4 hours at room temperature. Strain lemon rose syrup. *(Can be made 1 week ahead. Cover and refrigerate.)*

Fill cocktail shaker ¾ full with ice. Add vodka or gin, 2 ounces (¼ cup) lemon rose syrup, and a dash of bitters; shake vigorously. Strain into 2 small coupe glasses. Garnish with rose petals and a few peppercorns, if desired.

Classic Negronis

MAKES 2 COCKTAILS

Some of my happiest memories revolve around traveling to Italy in the fall. Quieter streets, lovely sunny-cool weather, the smell of truffles in every market—let me tell you, it doesn't suck. A pre-dinner ritual begins with a negroni, especially if we're in its birthplace, Florence. So anytime I am nostalgic for truffles—I mean Italy— I pour myself a negroni on the rocks, and it takes me back to those cobblestone streets.

A negroni is the perfect bridge drink from summer to fall because it's slightly heavier than the bright, iced cocktails of summer. Vermouth matters: Choose Punt e Mes or Sacred Spiced English vermouth, because they add notes of clove that hit the spot on brisk fall evenings.

    3 ounces (¼ cup plus 2 tablespoons) Hendrick's gin
    2 ounces (¼ cup) Campari
    2 ounces (¼ cup) vermouth, such as Punt e Mes or Sacred Spiced English (see Bar Tips & Tools, page 283)
    2 orange wedges or Dried Persimmon Slices (see recipe, page 273)

In a small pitcher, stir gin, Campari, and vermouth with ice; strain into 2 rocks glasses filled with ice. Squeeze in an orange wedge or add a Dried Persimmon Slice to each.

BAR NOTE: | My wintertime variation adds 4 ounces fresh orange or blood orange juice and replaces the persimmon slices with Dried Citrus Slices (page 273).

Fall Crudités with Hummus Duo

A colorful veggie platter paired with a delicious dip will never let you down. It's a workhorse for entertaining—a good platter looks gorgeous, tastes divine, meets the snacking needs of kids, carnivores, and vegans alike, and best of all, can be prepped ahead so you can actually enjoy a cocktail with your guests before the meal.

Prep your fall veggies—whatever looks good in your garden or at the market—by cleaning them well with cool water and a little scrub-brush action if needed. Dry well and slice with a sharp knife into bite-size pieces. Whenever possible, keep a little stem on your radishes, carrots, and turnips to make a little handle for easy dipping. If using a long bean or carrot, which would require two dips, cut them in half on the bias to discourage the temptation to double-dip.

Delicata Squash Hummus

6 SERVINGS

This hummus isn't made with chickpeas but rather with roasted squash. It has a similar texture but is somewhat creamier, and its flavor profile is buttery, earthy, and sweet. The garnishing with sumac brightens the flavors.

Winter squash is a funny thing. It's grown and harvested in the summer months and then put to cool storage until the fall or winter. Of course, you can eat it in the summer, but while it rests it turns more flavorful and gets sweeter. It's worth the wait.

2 small delicata squash (about 8 ounces each)
½ cup fresh lemon juice (from 2 to 3 lemons)
2 tablespoons organic tahini
2 garlic cloves
1 teaspoon cumin seed, toasted, ground
1 teaspoon Diamond Crystal kosher salt
⅔ cup extra-virgin olive oil
2 ice cubes
Sumac (optional; see Spice Drawer, page 274)

Preheat the oven to 375°F. Cut squash lengthwise in half. Pierce it a few times with a fork. Roast squash cut side down on a baking sheet until soft and the tip of a knife pierces the centers easily, about 35 minutes.

Cut stems off squash. Scrape out seeds. Scoop squash from skins and place in a food processor. Add lemon juice, tahini, garlic, cumin, and salt, and blend well. Add oil through the feed tube, stopping occasionally to scrape down the sides. Add 1 ice cube at a time and blend until totally incorporated (this cools the mixture and makes it super smooth). *(Can be made 4 hours ahead. Cover and refrigerate. Sprinkle with sumac before serving.)*

Garden Hummus

6 SERVINGS

Years ago, I was in a taxi in San Francisco with a Jordanian driver. I asked him about the food from his country, and he shared a tip for making the creamiest hummus—just add a few ice cubes to the blender. When I got home, I immediately gave it a whirl and it worked beautifully. A foodie version of *Taxicab Confessions*! The ice cubes cool the mixer, which helps keep the flavors fresh and make the texture silken.

I always reserve a few chickpeas from the can for garnish to show guests what the dip is and to also add some texture.

1 15-ounce can organic garbanzo beans (chickpeas), rinsed, drained, a few reserved for garnish
½ cup fresh lemon juice (from 2 to 3 lemons)
½ cup coarsely chopped cilantro leaves and stems
3 tablespoons fresh mint leaves, coarsely chopped
¼ cup water
2 tablespoons organic tahini
2 garlic cloves
1 teaspoon Diamond Crystal kosher salt
½ cup extra-virgin olive oil
2 ice cubes
Cilantro leaves (garnish)

Place garbanzo beans, lemon juice, cilantro, mint, water, tahini, garlic, and salt in a food processor and blend well. Add oil through the feed tube and blend well, stopping once to scrape down the sides of the food processor. Taste for seasoning. Add 1 ice cube at a time and blend until totally incorporated. Transfer to a bowl. *(Can be made 4 hours ahead. Cover and refrigerate.)*

Top hummus with reserved chickpeas and garnish with cilantro leaves.

Radish Tartine with Dill Butter

4 TO 6 SERVINGS

This simple appetizer is an elegant way to showcase the electric flavors and colors of watermelon radishes. If you can't find them at your market, consider growing some from seeds in your garden or in a terracotta pot. You can find the seeds online from Renee's Garden Seeds.

This dill butter can also be used to flavor other foods, like fish or chicken. I love thinly sliced, dense, northern European-style rye bread for this snack because the flavor and texture complement the butter and radish so well.

1 watermelon radish, very thinly sliced or shaved

6 tablespoons (¾ stick) cultured unsalted butter, room temperature

2 teaspoons chopped fresh dill

1 teaspoon flaky sea salt

1 teaspoon grated lime zest (from 1 lime)

Cayenne pepper

2 to 4 pieces thinly sliced European-style whole-grain bread, toasted

Fresh dill sprigs (garnish)

Scrub the radish with a brush to clean. Using a mandoline or sharp knife, slice the radishes as thinly as possible. Store in water until ready to use.

Mix the butter, 2 teaspoons dill, 1 teaspoon salt, lime, and a pinch of cayenne in a small bowl. Spread enough of the dill butter over each piece of toast to cover completely—don't be stingy with *le beurre*. Drain radishes and dry with a clean kitchen towel.

Arrange radish slices in overlapping layers atop buttered toast. Sprinkle lightly with sea salt. Using a long, sharp knife, cut the tartine diagonally in half or thirds. Garnish with dill sprigs.

Crostini of Drunken Figs & d'Affinois

6 SERVINGS

We have two varieties of fig trees, and both are in terracotta pots: Panache tiger fig (stripy on the outside and jammy on the inside) and Violette de Bordeaux (a mission-style fig that is fantastically sweet and rich). We use both types for this favorite fall appetizer, but feel free to use what you have on hand or find at the farmers market. It's beautiful, it highlights the season, and it's simple to put together. If you're gluten intolerant, just portion the cheese and figs onto the end of a treviso or endive spear, or use gluten-free crackers instead of a toasted baguette. D'Affinois is a wonderful creamy cow's milk cheese from the Rhône-Alpes region. If you can't find it, substitute with a triple cream like Mt Tam.

½ pound wedge d'Affinois cheese, room temperature

½ baguette, cut diagonally into ¼-inch-thick slices

Extra-virgin olive oil

Diamond Crystal kosher salt

8 to 10 fresh figs

2 tablespoons sherry, such as Oloroso from Jerez

2 tablespoons Sauvignon Blanc

Fresh mint leaves, thinly sliced (garnish)

Preheat the oven to 425°F. Remove d'Affinois from the refrigerator. Arrange bread slices in a single layer on a baking sheet; brush with oil and sprinkle lightly with salt. Bake until golden brown, 10 to 12 minutes. Set aside to cool.

Cut off the stem and neck portion of figs. Cut figs crosswise into $\frac{1}{3}$-inch-thick rounds and place on a plate. In a small bowl, combine sherry and wine, and brush onto fig slices. Spread the cheese on the crostini and top with the drunken fig rounds. Place the crostinis on a pretty platter. Garnish with mint.

Moroccan Lamb Meatballs in Lettuce Cups

MAKES 1 DOZEN MEATBALLS

Packed with wonderful Mediterranean spices, these meatballs have been a hit at many a dinner party. Adding sautéed shallots to the mixture keeps it moist—a handy trick I also use for my ground-beef burgers. Don't let the toasting and grinding of the spices scare you off—it's an easy step that completely enhances the flavor.

I make these often for entertaining because you can cook them before guests arrive, keeping them at room temperature until you're ready to serve. If you want to heat them up a bit, put them in a 200-degree oven for 10 to 15 minutes before serving. The meatballs are great on their own, but pairing them with my Cherry Tomato & Gin Jam (page 269) and labneh will take it to the next level.

MEATBALLS
3 tablespoons extra-virgin olive oil, divided
2 tablespoons minced shallot (about 1 small shallot)
1 teaspoon whole cumin seeds
1 teaspoon ras el hanout (see Spice Drawer, page 275)
½ teaspoon smoked paprika
½ teaspoon Aleppo pepper (see Spice Drawer, page 274; optional)

¼ teaspoon dried red pepper flakes
1 teaspoon Diamond Crystal kosher salt
1 pound ground lamb

PLATING
Butter lettuce leaves
Cherry Tomato & Gin Jam (see recipe, page 269)
1 cup labneh, thinned with water or lemon juice
Fresh cilantro sprigs (garnish)

FOR THE MEATBALLS: Heat 1 tablespoon oil in a small heavy skillet over medium-low heat. Add shallot and sauté until caramelized, about 10 minutes. Cool completely.

Over medium heat, toast all spices in a small dry skillet until golden and fragrant, stirring frequently, about 2 minutes. Finely grind toasted spices in a mortar and pestle. Mix in salt.

Using your hands, mix together ground lamb, shallot, and spices in a large bowl until combined. Using an ice cream scooper (2 tablespoon size), scoop out and form meatballs; place on baking sheet. *(Can be made 8 hours ahead; cover and refrigerate.)*

Heat remaining 2 tablespoons oil in a 12-inch cast-iron skillet (or other heavy large skillet), over medium heat. If you don't have a really large skillet, cook the meatballs in batches. Once the oil is hot, carefully add meatballs, spacing them apart. Cook until golden brown and medium-rare, turning occasionally, 2 to 3 minutes per side.

FOR THE PLATING: Spoon meatballs into lettuce leaves; top with a dollop of Cherry Tomato & Gin Jam and labneh. Garnish with cilantro.

Kabocha Squash & Red Lentil Soup with Yogurt & Mustard Oil

6 TO 8 SERVINGS

A one-pot wonder recipe that tastes even better the next day—what's not to love? This soup is a great starter and also hearty enough as a main course when served with Mini Pita Bread (see page 33) slathered in Whipped Feta-Piquillo Dip (page 32).

SOUP
¼ cup coconut oil
1½ cups coarsely chopped onion (about
    1 medium)
1 tablespoon minced peeled fresh ginger
1 tablespoon minced garlic (about 3 garlic cloves)
1½ teaspoons cumin seed, toasted
1½ teaspoons coriander seed, toasted
1 teaspoon curry powder
1 teaspoon mustard seeds
½ teaspoon turmeric
1 chile de árbol
2½ pounds kabocha or butternut squash, peeled,
    cut into 1-inch cubes (about 6 cups)

8 cups vegetable stock or water
1 cup dried red lentils, sorted and rinsed
¾ cup canned coconut milk
2 teaspoons Diamond Crystal kosher salt, plus
    more to taste
Freshly ground pepper

MUSTARD OIL
2 tablespoons coconut oil
2 teaspoons yellow mustard seed
2 teaspoons nigella seed
Plain Greek yogurt
Fresh cilantro leaves (garnish)

FOR SOUP: In a large, large pot, heat coconut oil over medium-high heat until hot. Add onion and sauté until caramelized, about 15 minutes. Add ginger, garlic, spices, and chile, and sauté until fragrant, about 1 minute. Add squash and cook for 2 to 3 minutes, stirring to coat with the spices. Mix in stock, lentils, coconut milk, salt, and pepper to taste. Reduce heat to low, partially cover, and simmer until the squash is fork tender, stirring occasionally, about 25 minutes. Remove from heat.

Working in batches, purée soup in blender. Season to taste with more salt and pepper. *(Can be made 1 day ahead. Cool, then cover and refrigerate.)*

FOR MUSTARD OIL: Heat oil in a small heavy skillet over medium-high heat. Add seeds and sauté until fragrant, about 1 minute. Pour into a small bowl to cool.

Bring soup to a simmer and ladle into bowls. Drizzle with mustard oil. Top with a dollop of yogurt and garnish with cilantro.

Chopped Waldorf Salad with Pomegranates & Whipped Cream Dressing

8 SERVINGS

My sister Patricia always makes this salad for our Thanksgiving buffet. It tastes like the whole fall season chopped into one bowl. Loved by kids and adults alike, it adds brightness and texture to the typically monochromatic Thanksgiving plate of food.

WHIPPED CREAM DRESSING
½ cup whipping cream
2 tablespoons mayonnaise
2 tablespoons raw apple cider vinegar
2 tablespoons honey
1 teaspoon flaky sea salt
½ teaspoon freshly ground pepper

SALAD
2 Granny Smith apples (unpeeled), cut into ½-inch pieces
2 Arkansas Black or Roma apples (unpeeled), cut into ½-inch pieces
1 cup walnut or pecan halves, toasted
4 large celery stalks, cut into ¼-inch pieces
2 Belgian endive heads, cut on bias in half
½ cup pomegranate seeds
¼ cup finely chopped fresh Italian parsley
2 tablespoons Meyer lemon juice (from ½ lemon)

FOR DRESSING: In a shallow bowl, whisk cream until it thickens. Whisk in remaining ingredients. *(Can be made 1 day ahead. Cover and refrigerate. Whisk to blend before serving.)*

FOR SALAD: Toss all ingredients in a bowl. Serve dressing on the side.

Butter Lettuces with Pancetta Chips & Gorgonzola Dressing

4 SERVINGS

This salad makes me so happy—it's like a BLT in salad form. With large-scale fall tomatoes, creamy dressing, and crispy pancetta, I don't even think about the bread. This gorgonzola dressing has been a staple in our house for years, and it doubles deliciously as a dip.

GORGONZOLA DRESSING
½ cup crumbled Gorgonzola
⅓ cup sour cream or plain Greek yogurt
¼ cup mayonnaise
2 tablespoons fresh Meyer lemon juice (from ½ lemon)
Flaky sea salt and freshly ground pepper

SALAD
3 ounces sliced pancetta
2 large heads butter lettuce (or 3 small), leaves separated
1 large juicy heirloom tomato, cut into 1-inch wedges
3 Persian cucumbers, cut in half lengthwise, sliced crosswise into ½-inch pieces
½ teaspoon freshly cracked pepper

FOR DRESSING: Whisk cheese, sour cream, mayonnaise, and lemon juice in a bowl to blend. Season with salt and pepper. *(Can be made 3 days ahead. Cover and refrigerate.)*

FOR SALAD: Preheat the oven to 325°F. Line a rimmed baking sheet with a Silpat (silicone baking mat) or parchment paper. Arrange pancetta in a single layer on the Silpat. Bake until crisp and brown, about 20 minutes. Transfer pancetta to a paper towel–lined plate to drain.

Arrange lettuce, tomatoes, and cucumber on a platter. Tuck in pancetta.

Drizzle with dressing and sprinkle with pepper.

Fall Salad with Quick-Pickled Persimmon, Avocado & Orange Thyme Dressing

6 SERVINGS

This creamy dressing (with no cream) makes scrumptious use of our prolific backyard oranges. French thyme is a bit woody, so it's easy to remove the leaves from the stem, while English thyme is soft and can be used whole, stems and all.

ORANGE THYME DRESSING
1 orange, peeled and quartered
½ cup extra-virgin olive oil
2 tablespoons Champagne vinegar
1 teaspoon Dijon mustard
1 teaspoon fresh thyme leaves
1 teaspoon Diamond Crystal kosher salt
½ teaspoon freshly ground pepper

SALAD
2 heads butter lettuce, leaves separated
2 little gems, leaves separated
1 Castelfranco or Treviso radicchio, leaves separated
3 avocados, sliced
Quick Pickles (made with persimmons; see recipe, page 271)
½ watermelon radish, very thinly sliced
½ cup pepitas, toasted in a dry skillet
Pomegranate seeds (optional)

FOR DRESSING: Use an immersion blender or a regular blender to purée all ingredients.

FOR SALAD: Divide lettuces, avocados, persimmons, and radishes among bowls. Drizzle with dressing. Sprinkle with pepitas and pomegranate.

Fall Tomato Salad with Dandelion Pesto & Honey

4 TO 6 SERVINGS

We have a beehive in our yard, and if everything goes according to plan (fingers and toes crossed), we collect a little honey in the fall. Once it comes into the kitchen, it goes fast! This is a fall riff on a classic caprese salad, a super combo of bitter dandelion greens, salty pecorino, bright tomatoes, and sweet honey. If you are looking for a change-up from mozzarella, seek out crescenza cheese from Bellwether Farms in Petaluma—it's creamy and delicious.

DANDELION PESTO

1 cup (packed) finely chopped stemmed
   dandelion greens (from 1 bunch)
¾ cup extra-virgin olive oil
¼ cup grated pecorino romano
¼ cup pistachios, chopped
1 garlic clove, grated
⅛ teaspoon cayenne pepper
Diamond Crystal kosher salt and freshly ground
   pepper

SALAD

4 large yellow heirloom tomatoes, or other garden
   tomatoes, cut into ½-inch-thick slices
2 balls imported fresh water-packed mozzarella,
   drained and torn
1 tablespoon honey
Flaky sea salt

FOR PESTO: Mix the dandelion greens, oil, cheese, pistachios, garlic, and cayenne pepper in a bowl. Season to taste with salt and pepper. *(Can be made 2 hours ahead. Let stand at room temperature.)*

FOR SALAD: Assemble the tomato slices on a platter. Place torn mozzarella pieces on top of the tomatoes. Drizzle with pesto and honey. Sprinkle with salt.

KITCHEN NOTE: | Tearing the mozzarella, rather than slicing, allows the cheese to come apart more organically at its natural fault lines, resulting in softer cheese that will more easily soak up other flavors.

Hope Ranch Mussels with Chorizo & Fennel

4 SERVINGS

This is a straightforward, beautiful meal using the bounty of our local Santa Barbara seas. It's great for entertaining or a busy weeknight meal because it comes together so quickly, and is fresh and flavorful (did I mention it's easy?). Serve it with Simplest Garden Greens (page 43) and warm, crusty bread to sop up all the delicious broth.

1 tablespoon extra-virgin olive oil

2 small fennel bulbs, sliced into crescents (fronds reserved for garnish)

5 ounces fresh chorizo

2 garlic cloves, sliced

3 pounds fresh mussels, scrubbed and debearded

1½ cups dry white wine

½ cup water

1 dried chile de árbol, chopped or ¼ teaspoon dried red chile flakes

Chopped fresh Italian parsley (garnish)

Heat oil in a Dutch oven fitted with a lid over medium-high heat. Add fennel, chorizo, and garlic, and sauté until sausage is cooked through, breaking up sausage, about 4 minutes. Add the mussels, wine, water, and chile. Cover, give the pan a shake, and cook until mussels open, about 3 minutes. Stir mussels; you may need to cover and cook for a few more minutes until they all open up. Discard any mussels that do not open.

Using a slotted spoon, divvy up the mussels, fennel, and chorizo into 4 shallow bowls. Strain the broth through a coffee filter or cheesecloth-lined strainer to remove any sand. Ladle the broth on top of the mussels and sprinkle with the reserved fennel fronds and parsley.

RAJ TELLS ME... A Grüner Veltliner would go great with these flavors; try the Sohm & Kracher "Lion" Grüner Veltliner from Weinviertel, Austria, or the Solminer Grüner Veltliner, Sta. Rita Hills.

Roasted Heritage Turkey with Thyme & Black Pepper Gravy

8 SERVINGS

The first time I made the switch to a heritage-breed turkey, I was afraid that my family would pummel me with cranberry-stuffed dinner rolls at the Thanksgiving table. I'm happy to report that they didn't—heritage turkey is here to stay. They do look different from pasture-raised turkeys: The breasts are smaller (don't judge), but they still provide plenty of white meat. The flavor is richer, the cooking time is less, and you don't need to brine in advance—simply smother with butter, stuff with aromatics, and bake in a parchment bag. I've used this method with birds ranging from 8 to 17 pounds, and each time, it turns golden brown while the meat remains moist. The rule of thumb for serving size is that the number of pounds in the turkey should match the number of people you're feeding. However, I always include an extra pound or two so there's enough for leftovers.

If they don't sell heritage-breed turkeys at your farmers market, you can buy them online; see the resource section on page 289. You can find unlined parchment bags at Whole Foods or online.

TURKEY

1 cup (2 sticks) unsalted butter, room temperature

2 tablespoons fresh thyme leaves, plus 8 thyme sprigs

2 tablespoons chopped fresh sage, plus 10 sage sprigs

3 teaspoons Diamond Crystal kosher salt, divided

1½ teaspoons freshly ground pepper, divided

1 10- to 12-pound heritage-breed turkey

1 extra-large parchment roasting bag

2 shallots, cut lengthwise in half

½ cup dry white wine

1 cup chicken or turkey stock

THYME & BLACK PEPPER GRAVY

1½ cups No-Stir Chicken Stock (see page 272) or other good-quality chicken or turkey stock

½ cup dry sherry

3 to 4 thyme sprigs

2 tablespoons cornstarch

2 teaspoons freshly cracked pepper

Diamond Crystal kosher salt

FOR TURKEY: Mix butter, 2 tablespoons thyme leaves, 2 tablespoons sage, 1 teaspoon salt, and ½ teaspoon pepper in a small bowl. Dry the bird well with paper towels. Run your hand between turkey skin and meat to loosen. Rub half of the butter between the meat and the skin. Rub the outside of the bird and bottom of the parchment bag with the remaining butter. Season the bird all over with remaining 2 teaspoons salt and 1 teaspoon pepper. Toss the shallots, thyme sprigs, and 10 sage sprigs in the cavity of the bird. Let stand 1 hour at room temperature.

(continued)

Position rack in lower third of oven and preheat to 325°F. Place a rack in a roasting pan. Place the buttered and stuffed bird breast side up in the parchment bag; pour in the wine and stock around the bottom of the turkey. Fold the end of the bag twice, inward—like your mom did on your sack lunch bag—and staple it twice to close. Place turkey in its bag on the rack set in the roasting pan and slide it into the oven. Roast 11 minutes per pound, about 1 hour 50 minutes for a 10-pounder. After 11 minutes per pound, carefully remove the bird from the oven and open up the bag along the fold so you can put it back in the oven covered if need be—scissors are a help here. Insert an instant-read thermometer into the thickest part of the thigh; it should register 165°F. Baste the turkey with the pan juices. If it has not reached 165°F, fold the end of the bag and return the bird to the oven, roasting until it reaches 165°F.

FOR GRAVY: Remove the turkey from the bag. Pour the contents of the bag into the roasting pan. Place over medium-high heat. Add stock, sherry, and thyme, and bring to a boil. Mix cornstarch with 2 tablespoons water and whisk into the stock mixture. Reduce heat to medium and simmer until thickened, stirring occasionally, 6 to 8 minutes. Strain gravy into sauceboat. Mix in 2 teaspoons freshly cracked pepper and season to taste with salt. Serve turkey with gravy.

RAJ TELLS ME... Try a Dolcetto for your turkey-day table, perhaps the Elio Altare Dolcetto d'Alba from Piedmont, Italy, or the Wilde Farm Dolcetto from Mendocino.

Quiche with Swiss Chard & Leek

8 SERVINGS

I love to make this exquisite quiche around the holidays in anticipation of houseguests—it's a wonderfully versatile dish to have in your back pocket because it makes for a stunning breakfast, a lovely lunch, or an easy dinner with a salad. The buttery crust helps hold the shape with nice, high sides. When blind baking the crust, make sure to fill the pie weights up to the very top of the crust; if not, it will sag.

Pâte Brisée (see recipe, page 272)

2 tablespoons (¼ stick) butter

1 large leek (white and pale green parts only), thinly sliced

1 cup chopped onion (about ½ onion)

1 large bunch swiss chard, center rib removed, leaves sliced (about 4 cups)

1½ teaspoons Diamond Crystal kosher salt, divided

¾ teaspoon freshly ground pepper, divided

2 tablespoons dry white wine

2 teaspoons minced fresh thyme

5 large eggs

¾ cup whole milk

½ cup crème fraîche

¼ teaspoon fresh ground nutmeg

2 ounces (½ cup) shredded gruyère or mozzarella

4 ounces soft, fresh goat cheese, crumbled

Brush an 8-inch round springform pan with 3-inch-high sides and a removable bottom lightly with butter. Roll 1 dough disk on a lightly floured surface to a ¼-inch-thick round. Cut the dough into a 9-inch diameter round and carefully transfer to the prepared pan, pressing the dough over the bottom and just slightly up the sides of the pan.

Roll the remaining disk out to a thickness of ¼ inch. Cut into 4-inch-wide strips. Brush the dough on the sides of the pan lightly with water to moisten. Press the dough strips horizontally onto the moist dough edges and wrap all around the insides of the pan, pressing firmly to adhere the bottom to the sides. Fold the top edge of the dough over until even with the lip of the pan. Gather the scraps of dough to use later for patching. Prick the bottom of the crust a few times with a fork and freeze the crust until firm. *(Can be made up to 1 week ahead. Cover crust with plastic wrap when firm. Cover and chill dough scraps.)*

Preheat the oven to 425°F. Carefully line the crust with parchment paper. Fill the crust with dried beans or pie weights all the way to the top. Bake until set and beginning to brown at the edges, about 20 minutes. Carefully remove the parchment and weights. Gently patch any holes in the crust with dough scraps. Continue baking until the crust is golden brown, 12 to 15 minutes. Cool completely. *(Can be made up to 6 hours ahead. Cover and let stand at room temperature.)*

Preheat the oven to 325°F. Melt 2 tablespoons butter in a heavy large skillet over medium heat. Add the leek and onion, and sauté until tender, about 10 minutes. Add chard, ½ teaspoon salt, ¼ teaspoon pepper, wine, and thyme to the onion mixture, and sauté until the chard is tender, about 5 minutes.

Whisk the eggs, milk, crème fraîche, remaining 1 teaspoon salt, ½ teaspoon pepper, and nutmeg in a large bowl until well blended. Add chard and gruyère to the egg mixture and stir to combine. Pour the filling into the crust; dot with goat cheese. Cover gently with foil and bake until the filling is set, about 1 hour and 15 minutes. Cool completely.

Run a knife around pan sides to loosen, if necessary. Release pan sides from quiche. Cut quiche into wedges.

RAJ TELLS ME... A chenin blanc would work very well with the quiche. Try an Arnaud Lambert Brézé from the Loire in France or the Combe from Stolpman Vineyards in the Santa Ynez Valley in California.

Indian-Spiced Cauliflower Steaks with Turmeric Cream

2 MAIN COURSE OR 4 SIDE DISH SERVINGS

One head of cauliflower with two components—this fall vegetarian dish is warm and cozy. The leftover pieces of the cauliflower steaks make the most delicious, versatile sauce. Cauliflower takes up a lot of space to grow, so I buy mine at the farmers market. Look for heads (or curds) that are tight fitting and unblemished.

1 large cauliflower head

2 cups water

2 garlic cloves

1 fresh bay leaf

1 teaspoon ground turmeric

2 tablespoons extra-virgin olive oil

Diamond Crystal kosher salt

1 teaspoon garam masala (see Spice Drawer, page 274)

1 slightly rounded tablespoon ghee or coconut oil

¼ cup golden raisins, soaked in hot water

1 small green onion, sliced

2 tablespoons chopped fresh Italian parsley

2 teaspoons lemon juice (from 1 lemon)

2 tablespoons sliced almonds, toasted

Place the cauliflower, stem side up, on the cutting board. Using a large sharp knife, cut the cauliflower through the stem into equal halves. Starting at the stem end of each half, slice cauliflower into ¾- to 1-inch-thick steaks, creating two steaks total. Break the remaining cauliflower into florets (you should have about 4 cups).

Place florets in a large, heavy saucepan. Add water, garlic, bay leaf, and turmeric. Cover and simmer over medium heat until the cauliflower is very tender, about 20 minutes. Remove the bay leaf. Place cauliflower (with its liquid) and oil in the blender and purée until smooth. Season with salt. *(Cauliflower steaks and purée can be made 1 day ahead. Cover separately and refrigerate.)*

Preheat the oven to 400°F. Sprinkle both sides of the cauliflower steaks with garam masala. Heat the ghee in a 9-inch cast-iron skillet over medium-high heat. Add the cauliflower to the skillet and cook without moving until browned on the bottom, about 4 minutes. Turn the steaks over, sprinkle with salt and pepper, and cook 4 minutes. Transfer the skillet to the oven; roast until cauliflower is tender and browned, about 20 minutes.

Meanwhile, drain the raisins and combine with the green onion, parsley, lemon juice, and almonds. Bring the purée to a simmer over medium heat, stirring occasionally. Season to taste with salt and pepper. Spoon into a serving dish. Top the purée with cauliflower steaks and spoon over the raisin mixture. Season to taste with salt and pepper.

RAJ TELLS ME... Go to the source: Friulian orange wine from Gravner Bianco Breg from Friuli, Italy, or Arnot-Roberts Ribolla Gialla from Napa Valley.

Chicken with Smoked Paprika, Meyer Lemon & Green Olives

4 SERVINGS

This is our go-to, simple weeknight family chicken recipe. Year after year, our Meyer lemon trees are super prolific, and I find myself using them in so many dishes. I love the mix of store-bought za'atar and smoked paprika with fresh, garden-picked oregano and lemons. We bake it all together in a cazuela (see page 278), and it turns out tender with crispy skin every single time. This recipe also works well with just chicken thighs, and it's delicious served over rice.

1 whole chicken, cut into 8 pieces

2 tablespoons extra-virgin olive oil

1 tablespoon za'atar (see Spice Drawer, page 275)

1½ teaspoons smoked paprika

½ teaspoon Aleppo pepper (see Spice Drawer, page 274)

1½ teaspoons Diamond Crystal kosher salt

1 Meyer lemon, cut into quarters

4 fresh oregano sprigs, plus more for garnish

½ cup green olives, such as Castelvetrano or Cerignola

Preheat the oven to 375°F. Toss the chicken, oil, spices, and salt in a large bowl. Transfer chicken pieces to a large cazuela skin side up. Nestle in lemon wedges (no need to squeeze) and 4 oregano sprigs. Roast chicken for 45 minutes. Carefully spoon any liquid from the dish over the chicken, then sprinkle with olives. Continue to roast until chicken is cooked through, about 15 minutes longer. Garnish with additional oregano sprigs.

RAJ TELLS ME... Try a food-friendly bandol rouge, like the Domaine Tempier Bandol from France or the Dirty & Rowdy Mourvèdre "Enz Vineyard" from Lime Kiln Valley in California.

Japanese Sweet Potatoes with Honey, Lime & Jalapeño

4 TO 6 SERVINGS

Japanese sweet potatoes are a perfect mix of creamy flesh and thin skins—no peeling required! The piquant sauce of garlic, ginger, and chile packs a punch, making it a welcome addition to the Thanksgiving table. After Turkey Day, they'll add pizzazz to a weeknight dinner of simple greens and a protein.

2 pounds small Japanese sweet potatoes, scrubbed clean

2 tablespoons (¼ stick) butter

1 tablespoon extra-virgin olive oil

1 teaspoon grated fresh ginger

2 garlic cloves, sliced

1 small fresno or jalapeño chile, sliced into thin rings

1 tablespoon honey

2 teaspoons fresh lime juice (from 1 lime)

1 teaspoon flaky sea salt, plus more to taste

Fresh herbs, such as wild arugula and cilantro (garnish)

Steam the whole sweet potatoes in salted water until cooked through and soft, about 30 minutes. Drain. Let stand until cool enough to handle.

While potatoes cool, preheat broiler, positioning rack 5 to 6 inches from the heat source. In a small saucepan, melt the butter over medium heat until foamy. Add oil, ginger, garlic, and chile. Simmer over medium heat until fragrant, about 1 minute. Remove from the heat and mix in the honey, lime, and salt.

Place potatoes in a large baking dish and squeeze slightly to open them up (my kids love to help with the smooshing). Pour the sauce over the potatoes and place them under the broiler until crispy and golden brown in spots, about 5 minutes. Keep an eye on them to make sure they don't burn. Sprinkle with a good amount of salt and fresh herbs.

Creamy Mashed Potatoes au Croquettes

8 SERVINGS

My Belgium-born mother certainly knows her way around the potato. It was a mainstay in her childhood garden and cold cellar ("kelder" in Dutch), making it a staple at most meals. She always tops creamy mounds of whipped potatoes (never made without egg yolk and nutmeg) with crispy breadcrumbs. Although she lives two hours away (three with Southern California traffic), I feel like she's in the kitchen with me every time I make one of her recipes. This is a particular favorite, especially for entertaining, because you can get away with making it in advance and still serve warm potatoes.

4 russet potatoes (about 2 pounds), peeled and cut into 1-inch pieces

3½ teaspoons Diamond Crystal kosher salt, divided

2¼ cups half-and-half

¾ cup (1½ sticks) unsalted butter

½ teaspoon ground white pepper

¼ teaspoon freshly grated nutmeg

1 egg yolk

½ cup panko breadcrumbs

¼ cup freshly grated parmesan

1 tablespoon chopped parsley

1 tablespoon extra-virgin olive oil

Place potatoes in a large pot and add 2 teaspoons salt and enough cold water to cover by 2 inches. Bring the potatoes to a boil over high heat, then reduce heat and simmer until tender, about 15 minutes. Drain the potatoes and return to the hot pot. Place over low heat and simmer until dry; mash with a potato masher.

In a small saucepan, heat the half-and-half, butter, pepper, and nutmeg over medium heat until butter melts. Next, whisk in the egg yolk. Slowly whisk the milk mixture into the potatoes. Season with the remaining 1½ teaspoons salt.

Butter an 8 x12-inch oval gratin baking dish. Mix panko, parmesan, parsley, and oil in a small bowl. Spoon mashed potatoes into the dish. Sprinkle with the breadcrumb mixture. *(Can be made 6 hours ahead. Cover and refrigerate.)*

Preheat the oven to 350°F. Bake gratin until the top is golden brown and heated through, 35 to 40 minutes.

KITCHEN NOTE:
I love a food mill, but I hate cleaning it, so instead I simply mash and stir the potatoes myself, and it comes together beautifully. If you want your mashed potatoes to be really creamy, use an immersion blender or push through a fine sieve.

Ciabatta Stuffing with Sausage & Sage

8 SERVINGS

The scent of onions and celery sizzling in butter transports me back to my childhood kitchen, working alongside my mom to prep Thanksgiving dinner with the pep of the Macy's parade marching bands on the television in the background. For me, the Thanksgiving meal is really about the stuffing; it's my favorite thing on the buffet.

You can't compare boxed stuffing with this recipe. It's spectacular—all the ingredients are great ones. You do have to make your own croutons, but trust me, it's worth it. Stuffing should be decadent and flavorful, with crispy bits mixed into a velvety smooth texture. Here, I add sausage to take it over the top. Yes, it's gilding the lily, but that's what the Thanksgiving feast is all about.

1 pound loaf ciabatta, cut into 1½- to 2-inch pieces

2 tablespoons extra-virgin olive oil

1½ teaspoons Diamond Crystal kosher salt, divided

¾ teaspoon freshly cracked pepper, divided

1 pound sweet Italian sausage, casings removed

¼ cup (½ stick) unsalted butter

2 cups finely chopped yellow onion (about 2 small onions)

2 cups finely chopped celery (about 4 ribs)

½ cup dry white wine or water (optional)

4 cups No-Stir Chicken Stock (see recipe, page 272) or other good-quality chicken or turkey stock

½ cup chopped fresh Italian parsley

3 tablespoons chopped fresh sage

Extra-virgin olive oil (for drizzling)

Preheat the oven to 325°F. Drizzle ciabatta with olive oil, ½ teaspoon salt, and ¼ teaspoon pepper on a large rimmed baking sheet. Bake until golden brown, stirring once or twice, about 20 minutes. Cool. *(Croutons can be made 1 day ahead. Let stand at room temperature.)*

Cook sausage in a large deep skillet over medium-high heat, until brown and cooked through, using a wooden spoon to break it up into coin-size pieces, about 10 minutes. Using a slotted spoon, transfer sausage to a bowl; reserve drippings in skillet. Add the butter to the drippings and cook over medium heat until foamy. Mix in the onion and celery, scraping up the brown bits on the bottom of the pan—if the bits on the pan are bordering on a scary brown color (like, burning), add wine (or water) to the pan. Sauté until the onions are translucent, about 10 minutes. Mix in stock, parsley, sage, remaining 1 teaspoon salt, and ½ teaspoon pepper, and bring to a simmer. Add croutons and toss to coat. Set aside.

Preheat the oven to 375°F. Smear the bottom of a large 2-inch-deep baking dish with room-temperature butter. Spoon stuffing into the dish. Drizzle the top with olive oil; this will keep the croutons from burning. Bake until heated through and the top is brown, checking periodically to be sure it's not browning too quickly, about 45 minutes (cover loosely with foil if necessary). Serve warm.

Grilled Purple Sprouting Broccoli with Tahini Dressing & Za'atar

4 TO 6 SERVINGS

If you're going to invest in a garden, grow something special. Enter purple sprouting broccoli, which is delicious, colorful, heat tolerant, quick to cook, and hard to find in stores. You can just harvest what you need without lopping off the whole head and then come back next week for more. It's like cut-and-come lettuce but with a brassica. If you don't have it in your garden and can't find it at a market, you can substitute small broccolini or broccoli head offshoots.

1½ pounds purple sprouting broccoli, trimmed

3 tablespoons extra-virgin olive oil

1 teaspoon Diamond Crystal kosher salt

½ teaspoon Aleppo pepper (see Spice Drawer, page 274)

2 teaspoons za'atar (see Spice Drawer, page 274)

Tahini Yogurt Sauce (see page 265)

Set a grill pan or comal over medium-high heat. Toss broccoli, oil, salt, and Aleppo in a bowl. Working in batches, add broccoli to the pan, creating enough space for the pieces to brown and crisp. Cook until the tops of the florets are crispy but not burned, turning once or twice with tongs, 5 to 7 minutes per batch. Transfer to a platter. Sprinkle with za'atar. Serve with sauce.

Agrodolce Red Cabbage

6 SERVINGS

This dish is easy to make and zippy in flavor, with a gorgeous garnet color. The tang from the vinegar, the sweetness from the apples, and the bit of heat from the chiles—damn, it's delicious. The clove, bacon, and apple seem to melt into the cabbage as it simmers. Plated with a simple pork roast or brisket, this is a winning side dish because it brightens up the mellowness of the meat. (*See photo of dish on page 168.*)

1 small red cabbage (about 1½ pounds)

3 bacon slices, cut crosswise in half

1 Pink Lady or Granny Smith apple, peeled, cored, cut into thin wedges

2 cups water

4 tablespoons raw apple cider vinegar, divided

2 tablespoons (packed) brown sugar

2 tablespoons red currant jelly

2 fresh bay leaves

2 chiles de árbol

4 whole cloves

1 teaspoon Diamond Crystal kosher salt

½ teaspoon freshly cracked pepper

Slice the head of the cabbage into 4 wedges and cut out the core from each piece. Next, slice each of those quarters in half, making 8 wedges total. Thinly slice the wedges perpendicular to the original cut mark, so you have a nice, even shred.

In a nonreactive Dutch oven, lay the bacon slices, followed by the apples and the cabbage. Mix together the water, 2 tablespoons vinegar, sugar, and currant jelly, and pour mixture over the cabbage. Next, add the bay leaves, chiles, and cloves, breaking them in half. Mix in salt and pepper.

Bring the cabbage to a boil. Reduce heat to low, partially cover, and simmer until cabbage is very tender, stopping periodically to stir and make sure there is enough liquid (adding water by ¼ cupfuls, as needed, if dry), about 2 hours. Add remaining 2 tablespoons apple cider vinegar and cook 30 minutes more to blend the flavors. Serve warm or at room temperature.

KITCHEN NOTE: Two little tips for keeping the cabbage colorful and bright. One is to add a little vinegar during the cooking process, and the other is to use a nonreactive pan. Carbon steel, aluminum, and cast iron are no bueno here—they'll change the color of the cabbage, making it dull.

Mincemeat Pie

8 SERVINGS

Mincemeat pie gets a bad rap; the name certainly doesn't help. Nonetheless, it's a long-held Thanksgiving tradition for my family; my father would be heartbroken if it weren't on the menu. As a kid, making mincemeat pie consisted of snapping open the can, spooning the contents into a prepared pie crust, and cooking until bubbly and brown. Okay, maybe I can see where that bad rap comes from.

I stand here today a little bit older and a little more discriminating, asking you to give mincemeat a try. This homemade version in particular is worthy of praise, and even though it may go against tradition, there is nary a morsel of meat or even bouillon in the mix. Fresh and dried fruit, nuts, brandy, honey, and a good pinch of salt make for a super flavorful pie.

2 small Granny Smith apples (unpeeled), cut into small dice

1 Envy or Rome apple (unpeeled), cut into small dice

1 cup walnuts, toasted and chopped

½ cup dried currants

½ cup golden raisins

¼ cup chopped dried Turkish figs

¼ cup freshly squeezed orange juice (from 1 orange)

¼ cup brandy

3 tablespoons honey

2 rounded teaspoons ground cinnamon

1½ teaspoons vanilla extract

¾ teaspoon Diamond Crystal kosher salt

½ scant teaspoon ground cloves

Pâte Brisée (see recipe, page 272)

1 egg yolk beaten with 2 tablespoons milk (glaze)

Sanding sugar or raw sugar

Mix apples, walnuts, currants, raisins, figs, orange juice, brandy, honey, cinnamon, vanilla, salt, and cloves in a large bowl. Cover and refrigerate mincemeat filling for 2 hours.

Preheat the oven to 375°F. Roll 1 pâte brisée disk out on a lightly floured surface to 14-inch round. Transfer the dough to a 9-inch-diameter fluted ceramic pie dish. Fold excess dough over so the crust has a thicker edge. Roll the remaining disk out to 10-inch round; cut out 1½-inch-wide strips. Spoon mincemeat filling evenly into the pie shell. Arrange 4 dough strips in 1 direction across the top of the pie, spacing them apart. Working with 1 strip at a time, arrange 3 more strips in the opposite direction atop the first strips, lifting strips and weaving over and under, forming a lattice. Gently press the ends of the strips to the edge of the crust to adhere. Press and crimp all around the top edge so that the lattice and crust are sealed together.

Brush egg glaze over the top of the crust. Sprinkle with sanding sugar. Bake for 30 minutes. Reduce oven temperature to 180°F and continue to bake until bubbly, 20 to 25 minutes longer. Cool slightly. Serve pie warm or at room temperature. (*Can be made 1 day ahead. Cool completely. Cover and let stand at room temperature.*)

Fresh Pear Panettone

MAKES TWO 7-INCH PANETTONES

Making panettone is easier than you would think, and I love utilizing the fresh pears that grace our trees in the early fall. This is a handy holiday-season recipe because it makes two loaves of bread, so you can keep one and gift the other. Any dried-up leftover slices make the best French toast (or since it's panettone, would it be called Italian toast?). Paper panettone molds are easy to find online or at most kitchen stores.

1 cup golden raisins

½ cup pear brandy or calvados

4½ cups all-purpose flour, divided

½ cup sugar

1 tablespoon active dry yeast

1½ teaspoons Diamond Crystal kosher salt

1 cup plus 1 tablespoon milk, divided

½ cup (1 stick) unsalted butter, divided

4 eggs, divided

2 Bartlett pears, peeled, sliced

1 cup bittersweet chocolate chips (optional)

2 teaspoons grated orange peel (from 1 orange)

2 7-inch paper panettone baking molds

In a small bowl, combine the raisins and brandy. Cover and set aside at room temperature for about 1 hour.

In the bowl of a stand mixer fitted with a dough hook, combine 1½ cups flour, sugar, yeast, and salt. In a small saucepan over low heat, combine 1 cup milk and ½ cup butter, and stir until the butter melts and the mixture registers 125°F. Add the milk mixture to the flour mixture and mix on medium speed until well combined. Beat in 3 eggs and then mix in the reserved raisins with its brandy, remaining 3 cups flour, chocolate chips (if using), and orange peel.

Put the dough in a large bowl greased with butter and cover with a kitchen towel. Place in a warm spot in your kitchen (I usually put it near my stove) until it doubles in volume in about 1 hour.

Generously butter panettone paper baking molds. Push down the dough to remove the air pockets. Turn dough out onto lightly floured work surface. Divide dough in half. Using your hands, shape one dough piece into a loose rectangle. It doesn't have to be exact here, people; it's going to be beautiful. Sprinkle pears over dough; fold in half lengthwise and roll into a slight coil. Nestle into a buttered mold, then repeat with the other half of dough in the second mold. Cover with a towel and let rise again in a warm spot in your kitchen until they double in volume, about 30 minutes.

Preheat the oven to 375°F. In a small bowl, beat the remaining egg with remaining 1 tablespoon milk and brush evenly over the tops of the loaves, avoiding any apparent pear. Bake until golden brown, about 20 minutes. Reduce heat to 325°F. Cover loaves with foil so as not to burn and continue baking until a toothpick inserted into the centers comes out clean, about 20 minutes. Transfer panettone to racks and cool completely. *(Can be made 2 days ahead. Cover and let stand at room temperature.)*

Kahlúa Bundt Cake with Cream Cheese Icing

8 TO 10 SERVINGS

I make this coveted family recipe every year for my husband's birthday. It's the dessert his vivacious Aunt Penny made in the summers when we would visit her on the Jersey Shore. Her recipe index card, in elegant script, calls for a box of devil's food cake, chocolate chips, and a cup of Kahlúa. This is a from-scratch version that's just about as easy as a box cake. No need to pull out your stand mixer—just use a few bowls and some elbow grease.

This recipe offers two icing options. Aunt Penny always made it with the Cream Cheese Icing, a total winner.

CAKE
1¾ cups all-purpose flour

1½ cups granulated sugar

¾ cup unsweetened Dutch cocoa powder

1½ teaspoons baking soda

1 teaspoon baking powder

1 teaspoon Diamond Crystal kosher salt

¾ cup buttermilk

2 large eggs

¼ cup safflower oil

2 teaspoons vanilla extract

1 cup Kahlúa

1 cup semisweet chocolate chips or disks

GLAZE
⅔ cup powdered sugar

⅓ cup unsweetened Dutch cocoa powder

⅓ cup Kahlúa

Flaky sea salt

CREAM CHEESE ICING
3 ounces cream cheese

¼ cup (½ stick) butter, melted

2 cups powdered sugar

1 tablespoon brewed coffee

½ teaspoon flaky sea salt

FOR CAKE: Preheat the oven to 350°F. Butter and flour a 10- to 15-cup nonstick bundt pan. Don't miss any spots. In a large bowl, whisk flour, sugar, cocoa powder, baking soda, baking powder, and salt. In the third bowl, whisk buttermilk, eggs, oil, and vanilla. Add the liquid ingredients to the dry and beat with a handheld mixer on high for 3 minutes.

Heat Kahlúa in a high-sided pot on the stove until hot and lightly bubbling. Pour into the cake batter and mix for 2 minutes. Mix in the chocolate chips. Pour batter into the prepared pan. Bake until a toothpick inserted near the middle of the cake comes out clean, 40 to 45 minutes. Cool completely, say a Hail Mary, and invert onto a rack.

FOR GLAZE (OPTION 1): Whisk all ingredients together in a medium saucepan and bring to boil. Cool to room temperature and pour over the cake.

FOR CREAM CHEESE ICING (OPTION 2): Whisk ingredients together and pour over the cake.

KITCHEN NOTE: If you don't have buttermilk on hand, mix 1 teaspoon of fresh lemon juice or apple cider vinegar into 1 cup of milk. Wait about 10 minutes. Voilà: buttermilk.

Persimmon Cookies

MAKES 24 TO 30 COOKIES

My friend Bernadette made a version of these cookies for us when I gave birth to daughter No. 1. They were so delicious that when No. 2 came around (luckily also born in persimmon-bearing months), I requested another batch and the recipe. They are cookies of the chewy, cakey variety; the persimmon pulp makes for an incredible texture: soft, round, and spiced to perfection. While the Fuyus are known to be crunchy and sweet, Hachiyas are meant to be consumed when completely softened and jelly-like in texture. Still, if you only have Fuyus, they will soften eventually in a fruit bowl and can be used here as well. Seek out walnuts from the farmers markets because they are far more flavorful than the store-bought varieties—and don't forget to toast them.

1 cup Hachiya persimmon pulp (about 2 large
    very ripe persimmons)
1 teaspoon baking soda
2 cups all-purpose flour
1 teaspoon ground cinnamon
½ teaspoon ground nutmeg
½ teaspoon ground cloves
1 teaspoon Diamond Crystal kosher salt

½ cup (1 stick) unsalted butter, room temperature
1 cup sugar
1 egg
1 cup golden raisins
1 cup chopped walnuts, toasted
Walnut halves or Dried Persimmon Slices
    (optional; see recipe, page 273)

Mix persimmon pulp and baking soda in a small bowl. In a separate bowl, whisk flour, spices, and salt. Using an electric mixer, beat the butter and sugar in a large bowl until very fluffy, about 5 minutes. Beat in the persimmon mixture and the egg. Add dry ingredients and gently incorporate. Fold in the raisins and walnuts. Chill dough for at least 30 minutes.

Preheat the oven to 350°F. Grease 2 baking sheets or line with Silpats or parchment paper. Using a small 2-teaspoon ice cream scoop or a mounded teaspoon, drop the dough onto the baking sheet*. Bake until the bottoms of the cookies are golden brown, about 15 minutes. Transfer to a rack and cool completely. *(Can be made 5 days ahead. Store in an airtight container.)*

* You can leave the cookie dough plain or press a walnut half or a slice of dried persimmon on the top just before baking to create a more finished look. The dried persimmon slice will almost cover the whole ball of dough, but the cookie will spread out beneath as it bakes.

winter

Winter:
Tamales, Parties & Planting for Spring

My husband is from upstate New York. After my first winter visit to a world covered in a blanket of snow, I gained some perspective on growing a garden in California. Let's just say I got a lot more thankful for the luxury of pulling parsnips and cutting celery in my flip-flops in December. Soft lettuces are nestled in with even softer chervil, fronds of flavorful fennel pop out of the dirt, and persimmons, guava, citrus, and pears are ripe and dangling from the trees. These are the holiday gifts this West Coast girl treasures.

Our biggest party of the year had humble beginnings as an early December dinner party with a few friends. It's now morphed into our annual Tinsel, Tequila & Tamales party for 100. The main table is laden with a variety of tamales (page 228) in large cazuelas alongside crystal bowls of warm ponche (page 205). With tapered candles, rustic food, and really fine booze, it feels perfectly Santa Barbara.

I look forward to the warm, earthy aroma of roasting chiles filling the house each December. The whole process of making tamales evokes the spirit of holiday togetherness; close friends, my kids, my kids' friends—we all sit around the kitchen, chatting and laughing, as we make hundreds of tamales.

In contrast, our New Year's Eve celebration is usually just with our nearest and dearest. We pop the Champagne and gather around the kitchen island eating crab legs (page 215) with our hands. Then we hit our home bar for more Champagne and gougères (page 219), and after midnight, I make carbonara (page 238) for everyone.

After the craziness and indulgent festivities of the holiday season, I love the idea of a fresh start in January. I renew my commitment to cleaner eating and less drinking and kick-start the exercise routine. Like most, I used to start strong, go hard-core for a few days, and then slip right back to the old ways. Over the years, I've learned to stack a few cards in my favor by preparing fresh-cut veggies every Sunday for the week to streamline cooking and give easy access to fresh snacking. We toss out or give away all the junk food from the house and move my lighter favorites into rotation (Winter Farro Market Salad with Sumac Vinaigrette, page 226, Wild Mushroom Soup, page 220, Moroccan-Spiced Pacific Red Rockfish with Green Olive Relish, page 240). It feels good to clean up our act, and, even better, it's wonderful to ditch my "comfy pants" by Valentine's Day.

Everybody wants to plant a summer garden, but a spring garden is really spectacular, and one of my wintertime joys is planting for spring. With such a wide variety of options, you can fill your garden and your plates with so many beautiful things.

WHAT TO PLANT NOW

Get planting just after the New Year, and while you're at it, it's a good time to prune your roses, too!

FAVA BEANS	SUGAR SNAP PEAS	FENNEL	GARLIC: CHESNOK RED GARLIC, TOCHLIAVRI GARLIC
LEEKS	GLOBE ARTICHOKE	CARDOON	ENGLISH PEAS
POTATOES: CARIBE, RUSSET, AND FINGERLING	GREEN ONION	GREENS: LITTLE GEM LETTUCE, BLOOMSDALE SPINACH, KALE	GOLDEN BEETS
RAINBOW CHARD	HERBS: PARSLEY, CILANTRO, CHIVE, OREGANO (WILD GREEK AND ITALIAN), BORAGE, PINEAPPLE MINT		PEPPERMINT, TARRAGON, AND DILL

Winter Recipes

Winter Drinks

1.

2.

3.

4.

Minty Ginger Green Juice

4 SERVINGS

The combination of flavors in this drink reminds me of a Moscow mule. It's a delicious and healthy option when you're on the wagon. I make a version of this juice blend year-round with whatever greens are growing in the garden, but my favorites are arugula, because of its zippy flavor, and mint, for its freshness.

2 cups chopped peeled pineapple (fresh or frozen)

2 cups (packed) arugula

2 cups water

2 ounces (¼ cup) fresh lime juice (from 2 to 3 limes)

¼ cup fresh mint leaves

1-inch piece fresh ginger, peeled

4 lime wedges (garnish)

Purée pineapple, arugula, water, lime juice, mint, and ginger in a blender. Fill 4 glasses with ice. Add juice. Garnish with lime wedges.

Arugula Gimlets

MAKES 4 COCKTAILS

This recipe calls for fresh lime juice. If you can, track down Bearss limes, which are amazingly juicy and flavorful, the lime equivalent of Meyer lemons. Also, wild arugula is remarkable in flavor and so easy to grow (seriously, plant some right now—it'll even grow in a pot on your patio). If your garden isn't cocktail ready, some fresh farmers market arugula will do the trick. It's dealer's choice when it comes to deciding between gin or vodka—both work equally well!

6 ounces (¾ cup) fresh lime juice (from 6 limes)

½ cup (packed) arugula, plus more for garnish

6 ounces (¾ cup) gin or vodka

2 ounces (¼ cup) St-Germain

Chilled sparkling water

Citrus blossoms (if you've got 'em)

Blend the juice and arugula in a blender or emulsion blender until the arugula is finely chopped; the color of the liquid will be a verdant shade of green. Strain mixture into a clean pitcher. Add vodka and St-Germain, and pour into 4 old-fashioned glasses filled with ice. Finish with a splash of sparkling water. Garnish with citrus blossoms and additional arugula leaves.

Cara Cara Margaritas

MAKES 2 COCKTAILS

I'm a sucker for anything pink, and I wait all year for Cara Cara oranges to dawn in markets. Usually spotted first in November and staying around all through spring, these seedless beauties are both tart and sweet. Personally, I'm running out of space in my yard, but they grow beautifully in our Santa Barbara hardiness zones. If you plant a tree, can we be friends?

1 lime wedge
Flaky sea salt
4 ounces (½ cup) fresh Cara Cara orange juice (from 2 oranges)
2 ounces (¼ cup) fresh lime juice (from 2 to 3 limes)
4 ounces (½ cup) tequila blanco
1 ounce (2 tablespoons) Cointreau
2 lime or Cara Cara orange slices (garnish)

Run a lime wedge around half of 2 rocks glasses and dip into sea salt. Fill glasses with ice. Fill a large shaker ¾ full with ice; add orange and lime juice, the tequila, and the liqueur. Shake it off—I usually count to eight in my head. Pour into the glasses, garnish with citrus slices, and serve. Cheers!

Ponche de Navidad with Guava & Hibiscus

12 TO 16 SERVINGS

This deliciously warm drink is perfect for any holiday gathering. Set out fireside, it's the showstopper of our annual Tinsel, Tequila & Tamales party. Use the prettiest bowl you have to showcase this garnet-hued *ponche* (punch). Brewed with cinnamon sticks, tamarind, dried hibiscus, and seasonal fruit like oranges, tejocotes, apples, and guava, this is a celebration of the winter fruit I find at our Saturday farmers market.

At our home, the punch bowl is always sans alcohol, so it's all-ages-friendly, and adults can doctor it up to their desired level of kick. Call an Uber and have fun!

10 cups filtered water
½ cup sugar
1 large apple, cored & sliced
1 navel orange, sliced in wheels
4 tejocotes, ends sliced off
3 guavas, sliced in half
4 tamarind pods, peeled, or 2 tablespoons tamarind paste
4 cinnamon sticks
½ cup dried hibiscus
6-inch piece sugar cane, peeled, cut into long, thin sticks, or 4-ounce package sugar cane swizzle sticks
4 whole cloves
1 bottle tequila, such as Maestro Dobel Diamante

Place water, sugar, apple, orange, tejocotes, guavas, tamarind, cinnamon, hibiscus, sugar cane, and cloves in a large stockpot and bring to boil. Reduce heat and simmer for 20 minutes to develop flavors. Strain into cups and then spike as needed with tequila. We fish out the sugar cane sticks to act as stirrers in each drink. If you have a large group, keep some punch simmering on the stove and refill the punch bowl as needed.

Black Manhattans with Bourbon

MAKES 2 COCKTAILS

This tastes like Christmas in a glass, so it's our go-to winter cocktail. Substitute the bourbon with extra añejo tequila for a delicious change up, and don't skip on the Luxardo cherries, which make it special. See Bar Extras (page 287). For more information on the Amaro and chocolate bitters used in this cocktail, see Bar Tips & Tools, page 283.

4 ounces (½ cup) bourbon or tequila extra añejo

2 ounces (¼ cup plus 2 tablespoons) Amaro Averna (an Italian digestif)

Chocolate bitters, such as Fee Brothers Aztec Chocolate Bitters

Luxardo maraschino cherries (garnish)

To make 2 cocktails: Fill a small pitcher or glass measuring cup ¾ full with ice. Add bourbon and Amaro, and stir to blend. Strain into 2 small glasses filled with ice, or serve neat. Add a dash of bitters to each drink and garnish with cherries.

TO SERVE A CROWD OF 6: Follow instructions above using 1½ cups bourbon and 1 cup plus 2 tablespoons Amaro.

ON CHAMPAGNE

TOO MUCH OF ANYTHING IS BAD, BUT TOO MUCH CHAMPAGNE IS JUST RIGHT.
— MARK TWAIN

Most of us can recall (rather hazily) those wedding receptions where we drank "champagne" or sparkling something-or-other that, come morning, left us with a headache the size of Texas. Do not let those experiences define Champagne. If your hobbies include collecting specialty sea salts and tracking down boutique butchers, then you should add Grower Champagne to your culinary pursuits. Actually, you should add it to your culinary pursuits regardless. Grower Champagne is a sparkling wine made in the Champagne region of France at family-owned vineyards. The families make the wine from the grapes grown on their own vineyards, in contrast to the bigger branded estates that buy grapes co-op style. Grower Champagnes go very well with all types of food because they tend to be drier in style and are well-balanced. Another bonus: You can find great bottles for less than the big brands.

I know wine-shop talk can get annoying; I've sat through my share of geeky/boring wine dinners. So I'll keep this simple and to the point. Below are five amazing Champagne choices recommended by Raj and enjoyed in our home with regularity. Whether rosé or white, they make worthy partners to your special holiday meals and Chinese takeout alike. These bubbles are great for gifting, too.

- CHARTOGNE-TAILLET
- SAVART
- JÉRÔME PRÉVOST (CHAMPAGNE LA CLOSERIE)
- BENOÎT LAHAYE
- CHAMPAGNE MARGUET (BENOIT MARGUET)

I DRINK IT WHEN I'M HAPPY AND WHEN I'M SAD. SOMETIMES I DRINK IT WHEN I'M ALONE.
WHEN I HAVE COMPANY I CONSIDER IT OBLIGATORY.
I TRIFLE WITH IT IF I'M NOT HUNGRY AND DRINK IT WHEN I AM.
OTHERWISE, I NEVER TOUCH IT—UNLESS I'M THIRSTY.
— LILY BOLLINGER

Bar Snacks

Bar snacks should be salty, stimulate the palate, and get your appetite ready. When it comes to cocktail hour, you won't catch me snubbing chips, pork rinds, corn nuts, or salted nuts of any kind. Here are a couple of my home-made favorites. You'll find another yummy option on page 124, Crispy Chickpeas with Ras el Hanout.

House Olives

4 TO 6 SERVINGS

I have made these olives for years. I love the buttery Castelvetrano olives from Sicily (see Bar Extras, page 287), but whichever you prefer, look for ones that are simply brined with no acids or added flavoring. Don't forget to put out a vessel for the pits. I prefer one that is metal, like a small julep cup or silver jigger that hides the pits, so you don't have to stare at the pit dregs after you've enjoyed your olives.

2 cups large green olives, such as Cerignola or
   Castelvetrano
¼ cup extra-virgin olive oil
2 fresh thyme or oregano sprigs, leaves removed
1 garlic clove, very thinly sliced
Dried red chile flakes
Flaky sea salt and freshly ground pepper

Mix olives, oil, thyme or oregano, garlic, and a pinch of red chile flakes in a bowl. Season with salt and pepper. Let stand at least 30 minutes and up to 3 hours at room temperature.

Popcorn with Za'atar

MAKES ABOUT 8 CUPS

There are so many beautiful varieties of popcorn available with varying texture and size. Even if the kernels are dark in color, they will still pop white. I like to use unrefined coconut oil for popping because it gives the corn a faint coconutty sweetness that complements the tart and earthiness of the za'atar. I don't miss the melted butter, but feel free to add a little if you'd like.

2 tablespoons coconut oil
⅓ cup popping corn, like mushroom or crimson
   premium
2 teaspoons Diamond Crystal kosher salt
2 teaspoons za'atar (see Spice Drawer, page 274)
¼ teaspoon Piment d'Espelette or Aleppo pepper
   (see Spice Drawer, page 274)

In a large pot fitted with a lid, add the oil and popcorn; give it a good shake to coat the kernels with oil. Cover and cook over high heat until you hear the popping noise. Reduce heat to medium and shake the pan continuously until the time between the kernels popping is more than 2 counts. Remove popcorn from heat. Add the salt and spices, and toss to coat.

GARDEN NOTE: Growing your own corn for popping is especially fun with the kids and something you can add to your garden in the late spring.

Herbalicious White Bean Dip & Crudités

4 TO 6 SERVINGS

This is such a nice, fresh alternative to hummus and makes great use of the soft winter herbs growing in pots. In the winter months I have dill, mint, and tarragon—a lone perennial and my favorite herb child—right outside my kitchen door. The easy access makes them a snap to elevate any dish.

2 tablespoons (packed) fresh dill or tarragon, plus more for garnish

2 tablespoons (packed) fresh mint leaves, plus more for garnish

1 15- to 16-ounce can cannellini beans, rinsed, drained

2 tablespoons Meyer lemon juice (from 1 lemon)

2 small garlic cloves, grated

1 teaspoon grated Meyer lemon zest (from 1 lemon)

½ teaspoon Diamond Crystal kosher salt

Dried red chile flakes

2 tablespoons extra-virgin olive oil

Assorted crudités, such as baby radishes, baby carrots, Japanese turnips, sugar snap peas

Add 2 tablespoons dill or tarragon and 2 tablespoons mint to the bowl of a food processor and pulse until finely chopped. Transfer the herbs to a medium bowl and reserve. Add beans, lemon juice, garlic, lemon zest, salt, and a pinch of chile flakes to the processor; blend until paste forms. Next, add the oil and blend until smooth (feel free to add a splash of water if the dip seems a little thick). Mix the bean mixture into the herbs. Taste for seasoning. Garnish with additional dill and mint. Serve with crudités.

Grilled King Crab Legs

6 TO 8 SERVINGS

Usually December weather in Santa Barbara is still pretty lovely, sunny, and cool. Our rainy season doesn't start until late January. So this grilled version of crab legs is a very doable appetizer for Christmas or New Year's Eve festivities. It's simple to duck out quickly to the grill with tongs and a jean jacket. If you can find split legs, it truly will make your eating experience so much easier and tidier. Or ask your fishmonger to split them for you. We all gather around the kitchen island with Champagne and feast on the crab legs with our hands. In SoCal fashion, I serve pickled jalapeños or fresno chile peppers on the side.

6 tablespoons (¾ stick) butter

2 garlic cloves, thinly sliced

1 tablespoon fresh lemon juice (from ½ lemon)

1 teaspoon flaky sea salt

Freshly cracked pepper

4 pounds Alaskan king crab legs, thawed if frozen, split

1 tablespoon chopped fresh Italian parsley

Quick Pickles (made with jalapeños; see recipe, page 271)

Lemon wedges (garnish)

Prepare the grill (high heat). Melt butter in a small saucepan over medium heat. Add garlic and sauté until fragrant, about 30 seconds. Add the lemon juice and salt. Season with pepper. Brush the meat of the crab lightly with butter mixture and sear meat side down for 30 seconds on the grill. Using tongs, turn so the shell is on the grill and baste with butter again. Close the lid and cook until warmed through, 4 to 5 minutes. Arrange crab on a large platter and sprinkle with parsley. Serve with remaining garlic butter, pickled jalapeños, and lemon wedges.

(Serve with any of the Champagne recommendations on page 209.)

Crispy Herbed Crackers

MAKES ABOUT 4 DOZEN CRACKERS

These quick-to-make crackers are awesome little bar snacks—versatile, delicious, and pretty, too. Instead of herbs, feel free to substitute with a mix of seeds (such as sesame, fennel, nigella, cumin, and pepitas). But don't skip the turmeric, which imparts great flavor and beautiful color.

1 cup almond flour

¾ cup finely grated cotija cheese

½ teaspoon flaky sea salt, plus more for garnish

½ teaspoon Piment d'Espelette or Aleppo pepper, divided (see Spice Drawer, page 274)

1/4 teaspoon turmeric

2 tablespoons extra-virgin olive oil

3 to 4 teaspoons water

½ cup fresh herb leaves and flowers, such as thyme, oregano, and cilantro

Preheat the oven to 350°F. Line a large baking sheet with parchment paper. Combine the almond flour, cotija, ½ teaspoon salt, Piment d'Espelette, and turmeric in a medium bowl. Mix in oil and enough water by teaspoonfuls until the mixture forms a moist dough.

Roll the dough out between sheets of parchment to the thickness of ¼ inch. Peel off the top sheet and scatter the herbs over the top of the dough. Replace the top parchment paper and gently roll the herbs into the dough. Cut into desired shapes using a flower-shaped cookie cutter, approximately 1½ x 1½ inches. Transfer cutouts to the prepared baking sheet. Bake until crackers are golden brown, turning the baking sheet halfway through cooking, about 10 minutes total. Cool crackers completely on the baking sheet. *(Can be made 3 days ahead. Store in an airtight container.)*

Cacio e Pepe Gougères

MAKES ABOUT 24

This is a basic French recipe for cheese puffs but with an Italian twist. Cacio e Pepe is a classic Roman Italian pasta dish that translates to "cheese and pepper." The combination of flavors is fantastic in these warm, buttery puffs.

In my travels through Burgundy, I was surprised and delighted by how large the size of the gougères were compared with the ones back home. I say go big or go home.

Traditionally, gougères are paired with Champagne (and really, who would want to mess with a tradition like that?), which makes it a perfect appetizer for occasions like New Year's Eve—or just any ordinary Tuesday. (See On Champagne, page 209.)

1 cup water

½ cup (1 stick) unsalted butter, cut into small pieces

2 teaspoons freshly ground pepper

1 teaspoon Diamond Crystal kosher salt

1 cup all-purpose flour

4 large eggs, lightly beaten

1 cup grated fontina cheese

1 cup grated pecorino romano, divided

1 egg, beaten (for glaze)

Cracked black pepper

Position rack in middle of oven and preheat to 400°F. Line 2 baking sheets with parchment paper or Silpats. Combine the water, butter, 2 teaspoons pepper, and salt in a heavy medium saucepan over high heat. Bring to a boil, stirring occasionally. As soon as the mixture boils, remove the pan from the heat. Add the flour all at once, and beat vigorously with a wooden spoon until the mixture pulls away from the sides of the pan. Return the pan to low heat and continue beating for 1 minute to dry out the dough.

Quickly transfer the dough to the bowl of a heavy-duty electric mixer fitted with a flat paddle. Gradually add the eggs, fontina, and ¾ cup pecorino, mixing at medium-high speed to incorporate the maximum amount of air, about 1 minute.

Drop dough by mounded tablespoonfuls onto baking sheets, spacing mounds 2 inches apart. If a point forms on the pastry dough, tap it down by smoothing it with your impeccably clean finger dipped in water.

Brush tops with egg glaze. Sprinkle with the remaining ¼ cup pecorino and cracked pepper. Bake one sheet at a time until the puffs are golden brown, 20 to 25 minutes. Avoid opening the oven door while baking, as humidity will escape and the cheese puffs will dry out.

To test for doneness, remove one well-browned cheese puff from the oven. Split it apart: It should be moist and steamy in the center. Transfer the puffs to a rack to cool. Serve warm or within 2 hours at room temperature.

Wild Mushroom Soup

4 TO 6 SERVINGS

I often serve this soup for parties as an appetizer in small demitasse cups. Earthy and tangy, topped with a dollop of crème fraîche, this is a wonderful, warm winter starter. I don't usually reach for a packaged ingredient, but porcini stock cubes from Italy add a great depth of flavor. Look for them online at Italian groceries.

2 tablespoons (¼ stick) unsalted butter

2 tablespoons extra-virgin olive oil

1 cup chopped celery (about 2 medium celery stalks)

½ cup chopped shallot (about 2 shallots)

2 garlic cloves, minced

14 ounces cremini mushrooms, sliced

4 ounces shiitake mushrooms, stems removed, caps sliced

2 fresh bay leaves

1 teaspoon Diamond Crystal kosher salt

¼ teaspoon freshly ground pepper

¼ cup Marsala

1 porcini stock cube

4 cups hot water

Splash of fresh lemon juice

1 heaping tablespoon crème fraîche (or sour cream), plus more for garnish

Fresh thyme leaves and chive blossoms (garnish)

Heat butter and olive oil in a heavy medium pot over medium-high heat. When the butter begins to foam, add the celery and shallots, and sauté for about 3 minutes. Add the garlic, and as that perfumes your kitchen, add the cremini and shiitake mushrooms and bay leaves. Cook on medium-high heat until the mushrooms release their liquid, stirring often, 5 to 8 minutes. Mix in salt and pepper. Continue to sauté until mushrooms turn slightly golden in color, about 5 minutes. Add the Marsala and cook for another 3 minutes.

Meanwhile, dissolve the porcini mushroom cube in 4 cups of hot water.

Add porcini water to the pot. Cover soup and simmer for 10 minutes. Before you purée the soup, be sure to remove the bay leaves! Using a handheld blender or regular blender, blend soup to desired consistency. *(Soup can be made 2 days ahead. Cool, then cover and refrigerate.)*

Pour the soup back into the stockpot on the stove set over medium heat. Once it begins to simmer, add a splash of lemon juice—a little goes a long way. Season with more salt and pepper, if needed. Add a heaping tablespoon of crème fraîche (or sour cream) to the soup. Whisk to fully incorporate into the soup. Ladle soup into bowls and drizzle with more crème fraîche, if desired. Garnish with herbs.

Braised Celery with Celery Panzanella

4 TO 6 SERVINGS

I am utterly obsessed with the flavor and texture of celery. It's so much more than just an accompaniment to onions and carrots. Diet fads aside, it can and should be the star of the show. For starters, it's an awesome addition to your winter garden because it's easy to grow, tastes amazing, is useful in so many ways, and is more complex than the store-bought varieties. Am I doing the hard sell or what? For this recipe, I braise the tender inner stalks and then top the salad with the sliced outer crisp green stalks tossed with croutons and a Meyer lemon dressing. I love this as a starter because it's a change-up from your typical leafy green salad.

BRAISED CELERY

4 cups water or No-Stir Chicken Stock (see recipe, page 272) or other good-quality chicken stock

1 cup dry white wine

½ cup fresh lemon juice (from 2 to 3 lemons)

8 garlic cloves, mashed

2 fresh bay leaves

4 fresh thyme sprigs

Dried red chile flakes

2 teaspoons Diamond Crystal kosher salt

1 teaspoon whole black peppercorns

12 to 16 inner tender celery stalks, both ends trimmed, cut lengthwise in half (reserve fresh leaves from the inner stalks for garnishing salad)

CELERY PANZANELLA

1 Meyer lemon, finely chopped (yes, peel and all, seeds removed)

2 tablespoons fresh Meyer lemon juice (from 1 lemon)

2 garlic cloves, grated

2 teaspoons fresh thyme leaves

½ cup extra-virgin olive oil

1 teaspoon flaky sea salt

½ teaspoon freshly ground pepper

Dried red chile flakes

8 to 12 outer celery ribs, cut in ¼-inch-wide, half-moon slices (about 4 cups)

Herb Croutons (see recipe, page 268)

FOR BRAISED CELERY: Bring water or stock, wine, lemon juice, garlic, herbs, chile flakes, salt, and pepper to a boil in a large high-sided saucepan. Add celery stalks; reduce heat to simmer and cook uncovered until tender, 15 to 17 minutes. Stir to move the celery pieces around as they cook so they are constantly submerged in the liquid, and skim off any foam that rises to the top. Transfer celery to a plate. *(Braised celery can be made up to 2 days ahead. Cool the braising liquid; return celery to the liquid, then cover and refrigerate.)*

FOR CELERY PANZANELLA: In a large bowl, mix chopped Meyer lemon, lemon juice, garlic, and thyme; whisk in the olive oil. Add sea salt, pepper, and a pinch of chile flakes. Set aside ¼ cup dressing. Add sliced celery and croutons to the remaining dressing in the large bowl and toss to coat.

On a platter, splay out the braised celery, then spoon over the reserved dressing. Heap the panzanella on top. Sprinkle with reserved celery leaves. Serve chilled or at room temperature.

Bitter Greens with Pears, Roasted Hazelnuts & French Vinaigrette

4 TO 6 SERVINGS

There are so many full-flavored greens that are often overlooked—and that are easy to grow, even in containers; use whatever you can grow or find at the market. As for the choice of cheese, this salad would honestly be delicious with almost any kind, even a wedge of soft Italian cheese like robiola (molto bene!) or an aged goat (très bon).

8 cups mixed torn greens, such as arugula, watercress, and treviso
2 D'Anjou pears (unpeeled), halved, cored, sliced
½ cup hazelnuts, toasted, very coarsely chopped
French Vinaigrette (see recipe, page 262)
Flaky sea salt and freshly ground pepper
Hard goat cheese, such as Spanish Garrotxa, or Italian cow's milk, like Piave, shaved

Toss greens, pears, and hazelnuts in a large bowl with enough vinaigrette to taste. Season with salt and pepper. Divide salad among bowls. Top with cheese.

Endive & Avocado with Cumin Lime Dressing

4 TO 6 SERVINGS

Even though I have a variety of citrus out back, I still buy weekly from Mud Creek Ranch at our Saturday farmers market (see Resources, page 289). They have stunningly tasty grapefruits, like the Oro Blanco, as well as pomelos and a fantastic array of avocados. Wherever you shop, if you can get your hands on a Pinkerton avocado, don't miss the opportunity to try one.

CUMIN LIME DRESSING
⅓ cup extra-virgin olive oil
¼ cup fresh lime juice (from 2 to 3 limes)
1 tablespoon unseasoned rice wine vinegar
1 teaspoon Diamond Crystal kosher salt
¾ teaspoon cumin seed, toasted, ground

SALAD
2 grapefruits
6 heads Belgian endive, quartered lengthwise
2 avocados (preferably Pinkerton), cut into wedges
Fresh chervil sprigs, coarsely chopped
Flaky sea salt and freshly ground pepper

FOR DRESSING: Combine oil, lime juice, vinegar, salt, and cumin in a glass jar. Cover and shake to blend. *(Dressing can be made 3 days ahead. Refrigerate.)*

FOR SALAD: Using a sharp knife, cut off peel and white pith from grapefruit. Cut between membranes to release segments. Arrange grapefruit, endive, and avocado decoratively on a large platter. Drizzle with the desired amount of dressing. Sprinkle with chervil and season with salt and pepper.

Winter Farro Market Salad with Sumac Vinaigrette

8 TO 10 SERVINGS

This is one of my very favorite salads to make in winter or spring. In fact, its versatility makes it a winner year-round—in summer months, substitute the fennel, snap peas, and radishes for cherry tomatoes, cucumbers, and sweet peppers (please wait until the summer months to use those beautiful tomatoes—it's worth it). There are many kinds of farro; look for the quick-cooking variety (semi-pearled cooks quicker than unpearled). If you're gluten intolerant, substitute quinoa for the farro.

2 cups semi-pearled farro

8 cups water

2 tablespoons Diamond Crystal kosher salt

1 fresh bay leaf

2 cups sliced fennel (about 8 ounces)

2 cups sugar snap peas (8 ounces), strings removed, sliced crosswise on bias

1 bunch breakfast radishes, thinly sliced lengthwise

1 7-ounce jar pitted Kalamata olives, drained, coarsely chopped (about 1 heaping cup)

1 cup chopped Italian parsley (about 1 bunch)

1 cup crumbled feta cheese (optional)

½ cup finely chopped fresh mint (optional)

Sumac Vinaigrette (see recipe, page 262)

Place farro in a large pot. Add enough cold water to cover and let soak for 25 minutes. Drain farro and return to the pot. Add 8 cups water, 2 tablespoons salt, and bay leaf. Bring to boil, then reduce heat and simmer uncovered until just tender but still firm to bite, stirring occasionally, about 25 minutes. Drain farro. Spread out on a rimmed sheet pan. Fluff farro with a fork and cool completely.

In a large bowl, toss farro with all remaining ingredients and vinaigrette. Taste for seasoning. *(Can be made 3 days ahead. Cover and refrigerate.)*

Tamales Two Ways
One: Swiss Chard Tamales with Rajas con Queso

MAKES 3 DOZEN TAMALES

Michoacan native Irma Aguirre, a longtime member of our household, showed me this special way to make tamales using the Swiss chard leaves from our garden instead of the typical corn husks. Not only do you get an extra dose of greens, but you can eat the whole tamale without unwrapping it on your dinner plate. My husband and kids are not exactly crazy about Swiss chard, but they all love these tamales. The moral: Don't give up on a vegetable—keep trying, and it doesn't hurt to throw some melted cheese into the mix.

The smell of roasting poblanos is so good that someone should bottle it. Most people think poblanos are on their way out of season as Christmas approaches, but they're still available at our farmers market, so I use them to make the rajas (poblano-based) filling for these tamales. I love the freshness of these green chiles alongside the dried and roasted red chiles in the pork tamales. In winter, fresh poblanos might not be very spicy, so add some green jalapeños if you want more heat. Serve the tamales with Ranchera Salsa (page 263).

6 poblano chile peppers (about 2 pounds)

2 tablespoons olive oil

½ large white onion, sliced almost paper thin

Diamond Crystal kosher salt

2 large bunches rainbow chard

5 pounds prepared masa dough

8 ounces Monterey Jack cheese, cut into ¼-inch-thick slices

1 package foil sheets

1 package deli parchment paper sheets

Roast the poblanos over a gas flame or under a broiler until charred and blackened, turning often with tongs, about 10 minutes. Run chiles under cold water and peel off the burnt skin (this stops the cooking process and helps the chiles remain toothsome). Cut off stems, then cut chiles lengthwise in half and scrape out the seeds. Tear chiles in slices (this is the old-school way of doing it) or slice with a knife into thin strips.

Heat oil in a heavy large skillet over medium heat. Add onions and sauté until translucent, about 5 minutes. Add poblanos and season with salt, and stir just until heated through. Set filling aside.

KITCHEN NOTE: | The rajas filling is also perfect for tacos.

Using a large sharp knife, cut 1 chard leaf along the stem in half and cut the stem out. Repeat with remaining leaves. Using a spoon or dough scraper, spread the masa in a ¼- to ½-inch layer on chard leaf, covering completely. Place 1 heaping tablespoon of the rajas filling in the center. Top with cheese. Fold the right side over the filling, then the left side over.

Place 1 foil sheet on the work surface; top with 1 paper sheet. Place 1 tamale in the center and wrap like a sandwich. This keeps the tamales moist during cooking.

Fill the bottom of a large pot with a collapsible steamer insert with enough water to reach the bottom of the insert (about 2 inches). Stand tamales side by side (straight up, shoulder to shoulder) in the steamer. Cover with a tight-fitting lid and cook over medium heat until tamales are firm to the touch, adding more water to the pot as necessary, about 1 hour.

Remove tamales from the steamer and let stand for 10 minutes. Unwrap foil and paper. Arrange tamales in a cazuela. Cover to keep warm and serve immediately.

Two: Pork Tamales

MAKES 3 DOZEN TAMALES

We have an annual holiday tamale party at our home in early December, and we make a lot of tamales for it (so it's handy that this recipe doubles easily). I do on occasion make the masa myself, but nothing I have tried beats the masa at my favorite Mexican bakery in Santa Barbara, La Bella Rosa (see Resources, page 289). We're fortunate to have many Mexican markets where I live, and that's increasingly true in many communities. They're a great resource for so many delicious ingredients, including the variety of chiles used in this recipe. Serve with Ranchera Salsa (see recipe, page 263) or guacamole.

PORK
2 pounds pork butt
½ large white onion, peeled
2 garlic cloves
1 tablespoon plus 2 teaspoons Diamond Crystal
    kosher salt
1 fresh bay leaf

RED CHILE SAUCE
2 dried ancho chiles, seeded
7 dried guajillo chiles, seeded

3 to 5 dried puya peppers, seeded
    (if you like it spicy, use 5)
3 garlic cloves
1 teaspoon cumin seeds, toasted
1 tablespoon olive oil

ASSEMBLY
1 package dried corn husks (you will have extra)
5 pounds prepared masa dough
1 package deli parchment paper sheets

FOR PORK: Place the pork into a large pot and fill with enough water to cover the pork. Add the onion, garlic, salt, and bay leaf. Bring to boil over medium-high heat, skimming the foam off the top using a slotted spoon. Return to a boil and cook pork for 10 minutes. Reduce heat, partially cover the pot, and cook the pork until tender, about 2 hours (make sure it's covered with liquid while it cooks and add more water as needed). Using tongs, transfer pork to a bowl; reserve 1⅓ cups cooking liquid. Using two forks or your fingers, shred the pork.

FOR SAUCE: Wash the chiles thoroughly and place in a pot of water over high heat. Bring to a boil and then turn the heat off. Let the chiles soak for 15 minutes. Drain the liquid. Purée chiles with 1 cup reserved pork cooking liquid, garlic, and cumin in a blender. Taste for seasoning, if needed.

(continued)

Heat oil in a heavy large skillet over medium-high heat. Add the shredded pork and stir to heat through. Mix in the red chile sauce and the remaining $\frac{1}{3}$ cup of reserved pork liquid. Taste for seasoning. *(Can be made 2 days ahead. Cover and refrigerate.)*

FOR ASSEMBLY: Pull corn husks apart, making sure to remove all the corn hair (the pelo). Soak the husks in hot water for 20 minutes. Drain and shake off excess water.

Before you spread the masa, some advice: Be sure to spread the masa on the smooth side of the husk (if you spread it on the bumpy side, the tamale will stick and fall apart as it's unwrapped). It's a little tricky—feel the husk carefully to determine which side is smooth and which side has ridges. Some husks will be smaller than others. Choose ones that span at least six inches at the base so you can fold it over. You can overlap 2 small husks together, using the masa as glue to piece them together into 1 larger husk.

Using a spoon or dough scraper, spread the masa in a $\frac{1}{4}$- to $\frac{1}{2}$-inch layer on the corn husk all the way to the sides and on the bottom, leaving the top $\frac{1}{4}$ of the husk untouched. In the center of the covered husk, place 1 heaping tablespoon of the pork filling. Fold the husk right side over the filling, then the left side over, then fold the top over toward you.

Wrap each tamale in the deli parchment paper like a sandwich. This keeps the tamales moist during cooking.

Fill the bottom of a large pot with a collapsible steamer insert with enough water to reach the bottom of the insert (about 2 inches). Stand tamales side by side (shoulder to shoulder) in a straight-up fashion in the steamer. Cover with a tight-fitting lid and cook over medium heat until tamales are firm to the touch and separate easily from their husks, adding more water to the pot as necessary, about 1 hour.

Remove tamales from the steamer and let stand for 10 minutes. Unwrap tamales from the paper and serve warm in their husks.

RAJ TELLS ME... You can virtually drink any wine with tamales (and we have), but something light-bodied is best, perhaps a Pinot or Nebbiolo.

Carbonnade à la Flamande with Parsley & Buttered Pappardelle

4 TO 6 SERVINGS

This classic, braised, sweet-and-sour dish is a winter staple in our home. It comes in handy on those days when you've got more work and kids' carpool routes to tackle than you do time. Similar to beef bourguignon but made with beer rather than wine, it can be served on fine china in front of a fireplace for guests or on the kitchen island for a casual family meal. Either way, it's comfort in a bowl. We especially love it when the weather turns chilly (yes, it does get cool-ish in Santa Barbara!).

STEW
3 pounds beef chuck, cut into 3-inch pieces
1 teaspoon Diamond Crystal kosher salt
½ teaspoon freshly ground pepper
4 tablespoons cornstarch or all-purpose flour, divided
6 ounces applewood-smoked, nitrate-free bacon, cut crosswise into ½-inch-wide strips (lardons)
4 large yellow onions, sliced
4 sprigs fresh thyme
½ teaspoon dried red chile flakes
4 garlic cloves, smashed
1 12-ounce bottle pilsner-style beer, such as Stella Artois
2 cups good-quality beef stock
1 fresh bay leaf

2 tablespoons raw apple cider vinegar or Champagne vinegar
1 tablespoon (packed) dark brown sugar

PERSILLADE
½ cup fresh Italian parsley leaves, chopped
3 tablespoons extra-virgin olive oil
2 teaspoons fresh thyme leaves, chopped
1 lemon, zested
1 garlic clove, grated
½ teaspoon flaky sea salt, plus more
¼ teaspoon freshly cracked pepper

PASTA
1 pound pappardelle noodles
2 tablespoons (¼ stick) unsalted butter
2 tablespoons chopped fresh Italian parsley
Whole parsley leaves (garnish)

(continued)

GARDEN NOTE: | Slow-cooked, fork-tender braised meat is always a good call for entertaining because you can make it a day ahead—in fact, it's usually more delicious when made in advance. It's best to cut the chuck yourself to get nice meaty pieces (store-cut pieces are often too small and disappear in the juices). If you're in Southern California, readily available tri-tip makes a great substitution for the chuck.

FOR STEW: In a large bowl, toss beef with 1 teaspoon salt, ½ teaspoon pepper, and 2 tablespoons cornstarch. Cook bacon in a large, heavy Dutch oven over medium heat until fat has rendered and bacon starts to crisp. Using a slotted spoon, transfer bacon to a small bowl and reserve. Place the Dutch oven with drippings over medium-high heat. Working in 3 batches, add beef to the drippings (be careful not to crowd the pan or you'll steam the meat) and cook until brown, 10 to 15 minutes total.

Preheat the oven to 350°F. Using a slotted spoon, transfer meat from the Dutch oven to a large bowl. Pour off all but 2 tablespoons of the drippings. Next, add the onions, thyme, and chile flakes to the Dutch oven and sauté on medium-high heat until onions are golden brown, about 15 minutes (browning the onions adds more flavor to the stew). Add the garlic and sauté 1 minute. Add the beer, stirring up brown bits from the bottom of the Dutch oven, and bring to a boil. Return the beef and any accumulated juices, bacon, stock, and bay leaf to the Dutch oven and bring to a boil, skimming off any of the impurities or foamy bits that rise to the surface.

Now make a slurry: Ladle ½ cup of the liquid from the Dutch oven into a small bowl; add the remaining 2 tablespoons cornstarch and whisk together. Mix the slurry into the stew. Cover the stew with foil, then a lid. Transfer to the oven; bake until meat is tender (the tip of a sharp knife should pierce center easily), about 1½ hours.

Mix vinegar and sugar into the stew. Taste and adjust seasoning. Return to the oven, cover, and bake 30 minutes longer to blend flavors. (*Stew can be made 2 days ahead. Cool, cover, and refrigerate.*)

FOR PERSILLADE: Mix all ingredients together in a bowl. (*Can be made 2 hours ahead. Cover and let stand at room temperature.*)

FOR PASTA: Rewarm stew over low heat while preparing the buttered noodles. Cook pappardelle in a large pot of boiling salted water until just tender but still firm to bite, stirring occasionally. Drain; return pasta to pot. Add butter and chopped parsley, and toss to coat. Taste for seasoning.

Portion noodles in shallow bowls; top with the stew and pan juices, then top with a spoonful of the persillade. Garnish with whole parsley leaves.

RAJ TELLS ME... Try a Brunello di Montalcino, like the Pian Dell'Orino Brunello di Montalcino from Tuscany, or the Leonetti Sangiovese from Walla Walla, Washington.

Midnight Carbonara with Champagne

4 TO 6 SERVINGS

This is a favorite late-night recipe after an evening of holiday party hopping. I've found that a little too much holiday cheer really builds up an appetite. We usually start fielding requests for this carbonara around 11 p.m., and within minutes my husband and I have welcomed an eager and hungry group of friends (in an Uber they come to our house) for some post-party carbonara and Champagne. This is quite possibly my favorite way to entertain: everyone gathered around the kitchen island, laughing and recapping the night. Our dear friend Chris Robles, who was not only a wonderful sommelier but an inspiring cook, taught me to use a heavy hand with the pepper. "Val, you can never have enough black pepper!"

After making this dish for years with everything from bucatini to rigatoni (don't tell the Italians), I've discovered that square spaghetti, with its square edge, holds onto the sauce and doesn't let it slip off like with classic spaghetti.

1 tablespoon extra-virgin olive oil, plus more

6 ounces ½-inch-thick slices pancetta or thick-cut bacon, cut into ½-inch-thick dice

½ cup finely chopped shallots (about 2 shallots)

2 teaspoons freshly cracked pepper, divided, plus more for garnish

¼ cup dry Champagne or white wine (plus a full glass for the chef)

1 pound squared spaghetti, such as De Cecco no. 413

2 tablespoons Diamond Crystal kosher salt

3 large eggs, room temperature, whisked to blend

¾ cup freshly grated parmesan, divided

Heat 1 tablespoon oil in a large, heavy, deep skillet over medium-high heat. Add pancetta and sauté until the fat begins to render, about 3 minutes. Next, add the shallots and sauté until pancetta is golden brown, about 5 minutes. Mix in ½ teaspoon pepper. Add Champagne and stir to incorporate all the flavors, scraping up brown bits from the bottom of the skillet. Set aside.

Bring a large pot of water to a boil. Add 2 tablespoons salt, then add the pasta. Boil pasta until just tender but still firm to the bite, stirring occasionally. Ladle off and reserve ½ cup of the pasta water, then drain the pasta.

Add hot pasta to the pancetta mixture in the skillet and, using tongs, toss vigorously over medium-high heat to incorporate. Remove from the heat and add the beaten eggs, 1 teaspoon pepper, and ½ cup parmesan; toss to combine. Continue to toss as you add the reserved pasta water, 2 tablespoons cheese, and ½ teaspoon black pepper. Don't worry: The residual heat from the pasta will cook the egg and the result will be succulent and delicious. Serve topped with more cracked pepper (that's for you, Chris), the remaining parmesan, and a drizzle of oil.

RAJ TELLS ME… So many delightful grower-producers to drink at midnight, or any time of day; see the list on page 209.

Moroccan-Spiced Pacific Red Rockfish with Green Olive Relish

4 SERVINGS

This is a simple dish to make but feels special because of the exotic spice mixture used in the marinade. If your market doesn't have rockfish, halibut works nicely. For a complete meal, serve with Coconut Carrot Purée (page 247) and Seared Bok Choy with Anchovy & Mint (page 251).

3 tablespoons extra-virgin olive oil

¼ cup whole-leaf herbs (mint and cilantro), plus more for garnish

3 garlic cloves, smashed

2 teaspoons ras el hanout (see Spice Drawer, page 275)

1 teaspoon Diamond Crystal kosher salt

½ teaspoon freshly cracked pepper

½ teaspoon sumac (see Spice Drawer, page 275)

¼ teaspoon cayenne pepper

4 5-ounce Pacific red rockfish or halibut fillets

2 tablespoons grapeseed or safflower oil

1 tablespoon butter, cut into 4 pieces

¼ cup dry white wine

1 lime, cut into wedges

Green Olive Lemon Relish (see recipe, page 264)

In a shallow bowl or pie plate big enough to fit the fish fillets, whisk together the olive oil, ¼ cup herbs, garlic, ras el hanout, salt, pepper, sumac, and cayenne; add the fish pieces and turn over to coat completely. Cover with plastic wrap and refrigerate at least 30 minutes or up to 2 hours. If the fish will be in the refrigerator for more than 30 minutes, place a bag of ice on the fish in the refrigerator until you are ready to cook. This will keep it super cold and fresh.

Preheat the oven to 325°F. Heat the grapeseed or safflower oil in a heavy, large, ovenproof skillet or cast-iron skillet over medium-high heat until hot (the oil must be hot in order for the fish to release and not stick to the pan). Brush off any herbs clinging to the fish. Using tongs, place the fish gently in the pan. Cook for 5 minutes (do not move the fish fillets; just leave them for 5 minutes so they develop a nice crust on the bottom). Turn the fish over using a fish spatula. Top each fillet with a piece of butter. Pour wine around fish; transfer to the oven and bake until fish is cooked through, 5 to 8 minutes. Using a spatula, transfer fish to plates. Garnish with lime wedges and more mint and cilantro leaves. Serve with relish.

RAJ TELLS ME... This would pair well with the Clos Canarelli Vermentino from Corsica, France, or the Ryme Vermentino "Hers" from Carneros, California.

Whole-Roasted Terracotta Chicken with Thyme & Za'atar

4 SERVINGS

What's more garden-like than cooking in terracotta? High heat and a terracotta roasting vessel make this chicken turn out delicious and succulent every time. It's perfect for a Tuesday-night dinner with the kids or when you're having grown-ups over on a Saturday night. I especially like it as an option for a meal to make for a family in need because: 1) it's delicious served at room temperature, so no need to reheat; 2) leftovers can be used for tacos, salads, or tortilla soup, so it's a nice addition when you don't know what else has been dropped off; and 3) it's not lasagna!

1 3- to 4-pound organic, free-range, air-chilled chicken	1 teaspoon ground white pepper
1 tablespoon Diamond Crystal kosher salt	½ cup (1 stick) chilled unsalted butter
	12 fresh thyme sprigs

Preheat the oven to 450°F. Rinse the chicken, removing any giblets. Pat chicken dry. Sprinkle all over with 1 tablespoon salt and 1 teaspoon pepper.

Carefully loosen the skin on the chicken breasts by sliding your fingertips between the skin and meat. Cut the stick of butter in half lengthwise and tuck each slice under the loosened skin of each breast. Put half of the thyme sprigs in the cavity of the bird and the other half in a 13-inch terracotta cazuela or small roasting pan (the thyme helps perfume the bird and also prevents the skin from sticking when you flip it over during roasting).

Place the chicken breast-side up on the thyme sprigs and roast for 25 minutes. After 25 minutes, turn the bird over, breast side down (I use tongs to make this easier). Be careful not to touch the sides of the cazuela with your fingers—ouch! Roast chicken for another 25 minutes. Using tongs, turn the chicken over again, breast side up, being careful not to tear the skin. Spoon any juices and butter over the chicken and season with a bit more salt. Place the chicken back in the oven and continue roasting until an instant-read thermometer inserted into the thickest part of the thigh registers 165°F, about 15 minutes longer. The chicken should be golden brown and smell divine! Serve warm or at room temperature.

RAJ TELLS ME... A red Burgundy would be excellent here, perhaps the Chanterêves Bourgogne Rouge from Burgundy, France or my own Domaine de la Côte Pinot Noir from California's Sta. Rita Hills.

KITCHEN NOTE: To add an exotic flavor boost, try rolling the butter in za'atar before stuffing it under the skin.

Lily's Paris Hot Dogs with Gruyère & Sauerkraut

8 SERVINGS

This hot dog came into our lives via a family trip to Paris. It seems funny to write "Paris" and "hot dog" in the same sentence. Well, during that trip, my husband surprised us with a fancy lunch at the Michelin-starred Le Jules Verne in the Eiffel Tower. It was so special to bring our kids there—then 10 and 12 years old—to enjoy the best view imaginable.

Expectations are a funny thing, aren't they? As excited as my husband and I were about the view and the prix-fixe menu, the kids were not. I don't think my youngest even touched her peach melba dessert (zut alors!). After she snubbed her meal, we headed down the elevator, and she bolted to a nearby hot dog cart. Tough love wasn't going to win this battle—we were on vacation, after all, and I have to say, that hot dog looked absolutely delicious! It was served in a crusty baguette, covered in melted gruyère. We all took a bite and decided that when we got home, this hot dog would have a place of honor in our dinner repertoire.

The key here is to use the best ingredients. Track down a good bakery for your baguette (buy them the same day you plan on serving them), switch out your normal hot dog for a nitrate-free, grass-fed dog, and grate the cheese yourself. Et voilà! Serve with Mustardy Potatoes & Celery (page 67) or Simplest Garden Greens (page 43).

8 all-beef organic grass-fed, nitrate-free hot dogs

3 fresh baguettes, cut crosswise into thirds (about 6-inch lengths) and split

2 cups coarsely grated gruyère cheese

Sauerkraut with Celery (recipe follows)

Dijon mustard

Ketchup

Score the hot dogs on one side, moving left to right and making diagonal cut marks about ¼ inch apart, then change the angle of the knife (90 degrees) and move right to left, making perfect cross-hatch marks. Repeat on the other side of the hot dog so you have marks on both sides.

Preheat broiler, positioning rack 5 to 6 inches from heat source. Heat a grill pan or cast-iron skillet over medium-high heat. Add the hot dogs and cook until the hatch marks blister and begin to open up. This creates a lot of nooks and crannies for the toppings and allows the skin to blister like it would on a barbecue. Place baguettes on a baking sheet and sprinkle with cheese. Broil until the cheese melts, watching carefully. Nestle in the hot dogs. Pass sauerkraut, Dijon mustard, and ketchup.

RAJ TELLS ME... Hot dogs with sauerkraut would be great with Duvel Belgian Golden Ale or an Alsatian white wine, like the Trimbach Pinot Gris Reserve.

Sauerkraut with Celery

MAKES ABOUT 3 CUPS

It took me a long time to get comfortable with the idea of fermentation, but I'm telling you, try it once and you will be hooked. Fermenting foods is a whole lot more simple than I ever imagined. Not only is this great for your gut health; the sauerkraut can last up to six months in the fridge. The addition of celery here gives this sauerkraut a more pronounced texture, which I love, and the mustard seeds make it ideal for our hot dog nights because you get mustard and sauerkraut all in one flavor profile. Maybe a New Yorker would even approve.

6 cups very thinly sliced cabbage (about ½ medium head)

2 cups thinly sliced tender celery stalks with leaves (about 6 stalks)

3 teaspoons Diamond Crystal kosher salt, divided

10 juniper berries

1 teaspoon mustard seeds

1 cup filtered water

Combine cabbage, celery, and 2 teaspoons salt in a large bowl. Using your hands, squeeze the mixture tightly and repeatedly until the vegetables release moisture and soften. Stir in juniper berries and mustard seeds. Transfer the mixture into a clean quart-size jar, packing the vegetables down tightly. Mix remaining 1 teaspoon salt into filtered water; pour over vegetables. Cover loosely and allow the mixture to ferment in a cool place, pressing down on the solids twice a day until the mixture bubbles and becomes sour, about 3 days for mild sauerkraut and up to 7 for a tangier version. *(Can be made 3 weeks ahead. Refrigerate.)*

Coconut Carrot Purée

4 SERVINGS

Every time I serve this carrot purée, people think it's butternut squash. Pick the smaller carrots in winter because they tend to be the sweetest. If shopping at the farmers market, sample what's available and select the best-tasting variety. At the supermarket, the most delicious carrots are organic and sold in bunches with the stems attached.

1 pound carrots, scrubbed with a brush (no need to
    peel), cut in 1- to 2-inch-long pieces
Diamond Crystal kosher salt
2 to 3 tablespoons canned coconut milk
1 teaspoon fresh lime juice (from 1 lime)

Place carrots in a heavy large saucepan with enough water to cover; bring to a boil. Add a healthy pinch of salt. Reduce heat to simmer and cook uncovered until carrots are fork tender, 13 to 15 minutes. Drain carrots, reserving the cooking liquid. Purée carrots in a blender with 2 tablespoons coconut milk and $\frac{1}{4}$ cup of the reserved cooking liquid. Mix in lime juice and season with salt. Add a bit more cooking liquid and/or coconut milk if it seems too thick or dry. (*Can be made 2 hours ahead. Cover, let stand at room temperature, and rewarm in pan over medium-low heat before serving.*)

GARDEN NOTE: If you're growing carrots, plant the seeds in sandy soil so the roots have an easier time of growing in a straight line, and thin them out when the first leaves appear. My favorite varieties are Tonda di Parigi (sweet little carrots that are round and quick to grow), Cosmic Purple, which are super fab for a crudités platter, and, for cooking in recipes like this one, Scarlet Nantes or Chantenay.

Romanesco with Rosemary Brown Butter & Parmesan

4 TO 6 SERVINGS

Chartreuse in color with stunning florets, romanesco has a sweet nuttiness and a gentle spice that blows the doors off of any other broccoli or cauliflower around. If you can't find romanesco, use cauliflower; sometimes even green varieties of cauliflower are available.

The brown butter and rosemary sauce here is also excellent on pasta. If you're so inclined, garnish with a sprinkle of thinly sliced shallot fried in grapeseed oil. *See photo on page 200.*

3 tablespoons Diamond Crystal kosher salt
1 medium-size romanesco, cut into florets, any large
    pieces sliced in half from tip to stem
$\frac{1}{4}$ cup ($\frac{1}{2}$ stick) butter
2 sprigs fresh rosemary
$\frac{1}{2}$ teaspoon flaky sea salt
$\frac{1}{4}$ teaspoon freshly ground white pepper
Parmesan shavings or coarsely grated (garnish)
Extra-virgin olive oil (garnish)

Bring a large pot of water to boil with 3 tablespoons salt. Add the romanesco and return to a boil. Cook for 3 minutes, then drain the romanesco, reserving $\frac{1}{4}$ cup of the cooking water.

Add butter and rosemary to the pot and melt over medium-high heat until it turns golden brown and smells nutty, stirring occasionally, about 4 minutes. Add the romanesco, reserved water, $\frac{1}{2}$ teaspoon salt, and $\frac{1}{4}$ teaspoon white pepper, and toss to coat. Transfer to a serving bowl. Top with parmesan and drizzle with oil. Serve warm or at room temperature.

Roasted Brussels Sprouts with Rosemary, Dates & Balsamic

4 TO 6 SERVINGS

My mother and I don't disagree about much, but how to cook brussels sprouts is one area of contention. Being from Belgium, my mom likes them boiled and tossed in butter, while this native Southern California girl prefers them roasted until crispy on the outside and soft and tender inside. The final touch—a drizzle of balsamic vinegar syrup and a sprinkling of chopped dates and hazelnuts—makes them sweet, tangy, and utterly delicious.

Even though I have a whole hedgeline of rosemary, which I love because it's evergreen and drought tolerant, it's not ideal for culinary purposes. It often gets too hard and pungent for cooking, so I grow some in a pot outside the kitchen—it has softer, newer growth and therefore more delicate flavors.

⅔ cup balsamic vinegar

6 tablespoons extra-virgin olive oil, divided

2 pounds large brussels sprouts (big golf ball size), rinsed, trimmed, cut lengthwise in half

1 heaping tablespoon fresh rosemary leaves

1 teaspoon Diamond Crystal kosher salt

Freshly cracked pepper

5 Medjool dates, pitted, coarsely chopped

¼ cup raw hazelnuts, toasted, cut in half

Flaky sea salt

Bring vinegar to a boil in a small heavy saucepan. Reduce heat and simmer until vinegar is reduced to ⅓ cup (liquid will be syrupy), about 15 minutes. Cool. *(Can be made 1 week ahead. Pour into a small jar and let stand at room temperature.)* You won't use all of the balsamic syrup for this recipe, so keep the extra and use it in lieu of aged balsamic vinegar.

Preheat the oven to 400°F. Place a large, heavy rimmed baking sheet in the oven until the pan is good and hot, about 15 minutes. Drizzle 4 tablespoons of oil into the pan. Place the brussels sprouts cut side down in the pan (be careful not to touch the hot pan sides). Sprinkle with rosemary and roast for 20 minutes.

Using tongs, carefully flip each sprout over. Drizzle the remaining 2 tablespoons oil over the sprouts, sprinkle with 1 teaspoon kosher salt and a few cracks of pepper (it's best to do this from a high vantage point so seasonings are evenly distributed over the entire sheet pan). Return sprouts to the oven and roast until brown and crispy outside and tender inside, about 10 minutes longer.

Sprinkle brussels sprouts with the dates and transfer to a shallow serving bowl, making sure to include the rosemary. Drizzle evenly with 2 to 3 tablespoons of the balsamic vinegar syrup and top with hazelnuts. Season with sea salt. Serve warm or at room temperature.

GARDEN NOTE:

Brussels sprouts take up a lot of real estate in the garden, needing a full 24 inches for each plant. (Lettuce and radishes can be happy underplanted beneath the brussels sprouts. You can also underplant herbs, especially mint, which will keep those pesky caterpillars away.) Four to six weeks before your desired harvest, lop off the top leaves of the plant. This will help it grow in a uniform way, yielding bigger and prettier sprouts. Just remember not to throw away those large leaves—they make a delicious snack. A bonus of growing brussels sprouts yourself is that both the leaves and stems are edible and can be enjoyed raw or in a quick sauté.

Seared Bok Choy with Anchovy & Mint

4 SERVINGS

Fusion food at its finest, this side dish highlights an Asian ingredient with an Italian sauce. Bok choy, a type of Chinese cabbage, is fairly easy to grow in the cooler winter months in California. I love its mildly sweet, slightly spiced flavor and its crunchy stems. Bok choy often gets pigeonholed as an add-in to stir-fry recipes, but it's delicious on its own drizzled with oil and sea salt and seared in a skillet or cooked directly on the grill. If you can't find it at the market, substitute small wedges of savoy or napa cabbage.

6 baby bok choy, cut lengthwise in half with stems intact, rinsed

7 tablespoons extra-virgin olive oil, divided

½ teaspoon Diamond Crystal kosher salt

½ teaspoon Piment d'Espelette (see Spice Drawer, page 275)

2 oil-packed anchovies from a can

2 garlic cloves, chopped

Flaky sea salt

2 tablespoons fresh lemon juice (from 1 lemon)

2 teaspoons unseasoned rice vinegar

Dried red chile flakes

Torn fresh mint leaves

Place bok choy in a large bowl; drizzle with 3 tablespoons oil, ½ teaspoon kosher salt, and Espelette; toss to coat. Heat a large cast-iron skillet or grill pan over medium-high heat. Add the bok choy, cut side down in a single layer; cook until golden brown on bottom, about 5 minutes (do not move the bok choy while it cooks). Once it's golden brown and crisp on the bottom, use tongs to turn the bok choy over. Turn off heat. Let the bok choy stand in the skillet for 3 minutes (the residual heat will continue to cook it). Transfer bok choy to a platter so it doesn't get soggy.

In a mortar and pestle, pound the anchovies, garlic, and a healthy pinch of sea salt until a paste forms. Transfer anchovy paste to a bowl; mix in lemon juice and vinegar, then whisk in remaining 4 tablespoons oil.

Spoon the dressing over the bok choy and season with sea salt, a pinch of chile flakes, and mint. Serve slightly warm or at room temperature.

Elizabeth Colling's Peanut Butter Cookies

MAKES 15 COOKIES

My lovely friend Elizabeth has a jewel box of a breakfast and lunch bistro in Montecito called Merci. A fantastic pastry chef and a former editor for Martha Stewart Living, she and I used to go for long jogs together, spending most of our budding friendship talking about recipes and food—multitasking at its finest. Ever since she shared this recipe with me a few years ago for her famous gluten-free peanut butter chocolate chip cookies, it's made regular appearances at our house. They're as easy to make as they are delicious. Elizabeth prefers the commercial grocery store peanut butter for these cookies instead of the healthy all-natural version she uses for sandwiches.

1 cup peanut butter (smooth or chunky)
½ cup sugar
½ cup light brown sugar
1 egg
1 teaspoon baking soda

½ teaspoon vanilla extract
¼ teaspoon Diamond Crystal kosher salt
½ cup bittersweet chocolate chunks or chips
Sanding sugar or raw sugar (for rolling dough)

Preheat the oven to 350°F. Mix peanut butter, both sugars, egg, baking soda, vanilla, and salt in a large bowl. Stir in chocolate. Roll tablespoon-size pieces into balls (I use a small ice cream scooper) and then roll the balls in the sanding sugar.

Place on a parchment-lined baking sheet and flatten slightly. Bake cookies for 10 minutes or until the edges begin to turn a golden brown. Remove from oven and let cool for about 5 minutes. Remove from the baking sheet and let cool completely on a wire rack. *(Can be made 1 day ahead. Store airtight).*

Pink Lady Tarte Tatin

6 TO 8 SERVINGS

I love a Pink Lady apple in general and especially for a tarte tatin because they're not too tart and not too sweet, and they maintain a good texture even after a long cooking time. I usually buy the White Toque brand of puff pastry because not only are the ingredients clean and pure (just butter, flour, and salt), but its round form fits in my pan without any trimming required. Serve with crème fraîche or vanilla ice cream.

- 7 to 8 large Pink Lady apples (about 3½ pounds)
- 2 tablespoons fresh lemon juice (from 1 lemon)
- 4 tablespoons room-temperature butter, divided
- ¾ cup granulated sugar
- 1 sheet of all-butter puff pastry, thawed and cut into 11-inch round

Peel and quarter the apples. Cut the core out at an angle of each of the quarters. Place the apples in a bowl and toss with lemon juice to prevent browning.

Melt 3 tablespoons butter in a 10-inch ovenproof skillet over medium heat, swirling to coat bottom. Pour the sugar over the butter and continue to cook until the sugar melts and the mixture is golden brown, swirling occasionally (do not stir), about 15 minutes.

Preheat the oven to 375°F. Remove the skillet from the heat. Arrange apples rounded side down over the caramel, starting on the outside and working toward the center in concentric circles (apples should cover the bottom of the pan; nestle them in as snugly as possible). Reserve remaining apple quarters. Make it pretty, as the bottom will become the top of the tart when turned out. Place the skillet back on the stove over medium heat. Cover and cook until apples are tender and caramel darkens in color, about 30 minutes (apples will shrink as their juices are released, so as space opens up, add the remaining apple quarters).

Next, place the thawed puff pastry over the apples and tuck the ends down the side of the pan. Prick the dough using a fork (this doesn't have to be perfect, but be careful because the pan is hot).

Using oven mitts, transfer the skillet to the oven. Bake until the crust is golden brown and caramel is bubbling at sides, about 35 minutes. Remove from the oven and let tart cool in the skillet for 10 to 15 minutes to allow the caramel to thicken a bit. Invert a heat-proof platter over the tart. Using oven mitts, firmly grasp the platter and sides of the skillet together and flip over in one quick motion, releasing tart onto plate. Cool slightly or up to 2 hours.

RAJ TELLS ME... With the apple tart, try a late-harvest Chenin Blanc, like the Domaine des Baumard Quarts de Chaume from the Loire, France.

Chocolate, Coconut & Almond Tart

10 TO 12 SERVINGS

This tart tastes just like an Almond Joy. Chewy, chocolaty, and crunchy, it's an awesome dessert to offer if your guests have food restrictions—it tastes like absolutely nothing is missing but just happens to be free of both gluten and dairy. Canned unsweetened coconut cream is a luscious non-dairy thickener when mixed into coffee or cocktails. (It's not, however, to be confused with Coco Lopez, a canned cream of coconut that is super sweet and used to make piña coladas.)

CRUST

1 cup sliced raw almonds

1 cup unsweetened shredded coconut

⅓ cup sugar

¼ cup blanched almond flour or coconut flour

3 tablespoons unsweetened cocoa powder

¼ teaspoon fine sea salt

3 tablespoons unrefined coconut oil, warmed if solid

2 tablespoons canned unsweetened coconut cream

FILLING

1 cup unsweetened shredded coconut

½ cup canned unsweetened coconut cream

¼ cup sugar

TOPPING

½ cup canned unsweetened coconut cream

¼ cup unrefined coconut oil

1 cup bittersweet chocolate chips, such as Pascha or Callebaut

⅛ teaspoon fine sea salt

Flaky sea salt for sprinkling

FOR CRUST: Preheat the oven to 375°F. Combine the almonds and coconut on a heavy rimmed baking sheet. Toast in the oven until the almonds and coconut are just beginning to turn golden brown, stirring occasionally, about 6 minutes. Cool completely. (Maintain oven temperature.)

Transfer the almonds and coconut to a food processor. Add the sugar, almond flour, cocoa powder, and salt, and pulse until the nuts are finely chopped. Pour in the coconut oil and coconut cream, and process until moist crumbs form. Press the dough evenly over the bottom and up sides of a 13x4-inch rectangular tart pan with a removable bottom. Bake until just beginning to turn golden brown at the edges, about 10 minutes. Cool.

FOR FILLING: Stir the shredded coconut, coconut cream, and sugar to blend in a heavy small saucepan. Simmer rapidly over medium heat until the liquid is reduced to coat the coconut thickly, stirring frequently, about 5 minutes. Cool slightly, then carefully spread warm filling evenly over the bottom of the crust.

FOR TOPPING: Bring the coconut cream and coconut oil to a simmer in a heavy medium saucepan. Remove from heat; add the chocolate and ⅛ teaspoon salt and whisk until the chocolate melts and the mixture is smooth. Pour the chocolate mixture over the coconut layer and smooth the top. Sprinkle the tart lightly with flaky sea salt. Chill until chocolate is set, about 4 hours. *(Tart can be made up to 2 days ahead. Cover; keep chilled.)*

Individual Sticky Date Puddings

8 SERVINGS

Living in California, we are lucky enough to have beautiful dates gracing our wintertime farmers markets. I can't look at a date without thinking about family vacations to Palm Desert and passing Hadley's Market lined with wooden crates of dried fruit and nuts and the best date shakes on the planet. I still dream about those shakes, and I'll look for any opportunity to incorporate dates into a recipe (see Roasted Brussels Sprouts with Rosemary, Dates & Balsamic, page 248).

I love this dessert for entertaining because you can make it in advance and then just reheat the puddings in their ramekins and turn them out onto a pretty plate. The "pudding" is really a moist date cake cloaked in a rich caramel sauce, which makes for one of the best combos ever. Chewy, gooey, yummy, warm… It's one of those rare recipes that's simple to make but stops everyone in their tracks after the first bite. You'll need eight 6-ounce oven-safe ramekins to make the individual portions or a pretty baking dish so you can serve it tableside.

CARAMEL SAUCE
½ cup (1 stick) unsalted butter
½ cup (packed) dark brown sugar
1½ cups whipping cream
1 tablespoon whiskey, bourbon or rye
1 teaspoon vanilla extract
1 teaspoon flaky sea salt

PUDDING
1 cup packed pitted Medjool dates, about 10
1 cup hot water
1 cup all-purpose flour
¾ cup (packed) golden brown sugar

2 eggs
3 tablespoons cold unsalted butter
1 tablespoon molasses
1 tablespoon whiskey, bourbon or rye
1 teaspoon vanilla extract
1 teaspoon baking soda
1 teaspoon Diamond Crystal kosher salt

PLATING
Flaky sea salt
Crème fraîche (optional)
Additional chopped, pitted dates (garnish)

FOR SAUCE: Melt the butter and sugar together in a heavy medium saucepan over medium heat. Once melted, slowly add the cream, whisking as you go to incorporate. Make sure you do this step slowly; otherwise, your butter and cream will separate (trust me, I know from experience). Bring the mixture to a light bubble and add whiskey, vanilla, salt, and maybe even an extra splash of whiskey—your choice. Simmer until the sauce begins to thicken and coats the back of a spoon, stirring occasionally, 5 to 8 minutes. You should have a scant 2 cups. *(Can be made 3 days ahead. Cover and refrigerate.)*

(continued)

FOR PUDDING: Preheat the oven to 350°F. Generously butter bottom and sides of eight ½-cup ramekins. Put the dates and hot water in a bowl; allow to soak until the dates soften, about 15 minutes.

Drain the dates, reserving ⅓ cup of the water. In a food processor, blend flour, brown sugar, eggs, butter, molasses, whiskey, vanilla, baking soda, and salt and pulse until smooth. Next, add the dates and ⅓ cup reserved water, and blend until flecks of the dates are integrated into the batter.

Fill each prepared ramekin halfway with batter, about ¼ cup in each. Place the ramekins into a high-sided roasting pan or casserole dish; you might have to use two baking pans to fit the 8 ramekins. After placing the ramekins in the pan or dish, fill it a quarter way up the ramekins with hot water. The easiest way to do this is to pour hot water from a kettle straight into the pan and gingerly slide it in the oven. Bake until a tester inserted into the center of the cakes comes out clean, about 20 minutes.

Rewarm caramel sauce. Prick each warm pudding a few times with a toothpick and drizzle 1 tablespoon of sauce over each. (*Can be made 4 hours ahead. Cool completely.*)

Preheat broiler, positioning rack 5 to 6 inches from heat source. Rewarm sauce; drizzle another 1 tablespoon of sauce over each pudding. Place the ramekins under the broiler and broil until heated through, about 5 minutes (the edges will darken a bit, which will add to the texture of the dessert).

FOR PLATING: Turn the ramekins out into a shallow bowl or onto a plate, and pour another 1 to 2 tablespoons of warm caramel sauce over each. Sprinkle with a pinch of sea salt. Top with a dollop of crème fraîche if desired. Garnish with chopped dates.

RAJ TELLS ME... This is an excellent opportunity to drink whatever tawny port you might have in your bar. I like the Niepoort 10 Year Tawny Port from Porto, Portugal.

Pantry Recipes & Gifts from the Garden

In this chapter, I detail the recipes that I use on repeat regardless of the season—things like salsas, sauces, killer dressings, and relishes. I also share my go-to gifts from the garden that I give friends and family when I'm staring down a bumper crop of garden booty—or am just in the mood to whip up a homemade gift. Package the chips, rimming salt, citrus slices, pâte brisée, or granola in cellophane bags tied with a pretty ribbon and a sprig from the garden, and you've got the perfect hostess gift. And when put into cute mason jars, many of the salsas, jams, pickles, and dressings in the coming pages make awesome gifts, too.

DRESSINGS & SALSAS

Spicy Thousand Island

MAKES ABOUT 1½ CUPS

This old-school salad dressing is zippy and delicious. It also doubles as our "special sauce" on burger night.

½ cup mayonnaise
½ cup ketchup
2 tablespoons Dijon mustard, grainy or smooth
12 cornichon pickles, minced
1 tablespoon cornichon pickle juice
1 tablespoon fresh lemon juice (from ½ lemon)
2 teaspoons Worcestershire sauce
¼ to ½ teaspoon Tabasco hot sauce
½ teaspoon Diamond Crystal kosher salt
¼ teaspoon freshly cracked pepper

Mix all ingredients in a bowl. *(Can be made 3 days ahead. Cover and refrigerate.)*

French Vinaigrette

MAKES ABOUT ¾ CUP

2 tablespoons sherry vinegar
2 tablespoons fresh lemon juice (from 1 lemon)
2 teaspoons Dijon mustard
1 teaspoon Diamond Crystal kosher salt
1 teaspoon freshly ground pepper
½ cup extra-virgin olive oil

Whisk vinegar, lemon juice, mustard, salt, and pepper in a large bowl; gradually whisk in oil. *(Can be made 1 week ahead; cover and refrigerate.)*

Sumac Vinaigrette

MAKES ABOUT 1 CUP

Equally as delicious on grain salads as it is on leafy greens.

⅔ cup extra-virgin olive oil
¼ cup red wine vinegar
1 tablespoon fresh lemon juice (from ½ lemon)
1 teaspoon Diamond Crystal kosher salt
½ teaspoon sumac (see Spice Drawer, page 275)
¼ teaspoon freshly cracked pepper

Combine all ingredients in a jar; cover and shake to blend. *(Can be made 1 day ahead. Cover and refrigerate.)*

Roasted Garden Salsa *(pictured on page 117)*

MAKES ABOUT 2 CUPS

The spiciness of the salsa depends on the heat of the pepper, so make sure you taste the pepper before you use it, and know that its heat gets stronger at the stem. I look for jalapeños with scars or fine lines on them, which is usually a sign that the pepper has good heat structure. (If your jalapeños are really mild, consider adding one serrano per two jalapeños—you'll get a nice pepper flavor along with the kick from the serrano.) I add a variety of tomatoes to my salsas for consistency and flavor; without the variety, the sauce becomes either too runny (if using only vine-ripe) or too coagulated (if using only plum tomatoes).

2 medium vine-ripened tomatoes (10 to 12 ounces)
2 Roma tomatoes (8 to 10 ounces)
2 jalapeño chiles
¼ white or yellow onion
1 large garlic clove
½ teaspoon flaky sea salt
1 tablespoon chopped fresh cilantro

Roast tomatoes, jalapeños, and onion wedge directly on gas burners or broil on a sheet pan in the oven for about 5 minutes, using tongs to turn vegetables occasionally for even blistering and blackening of the skins.

Cool vegetables slightly. Peel jalapeños, then slice in half; discard stems and seeds. In a mortar and pestle, pound garlic and salt, and then the jalapeños. Transfer the mixture to a bowl.

Chop the tomatoes (it's okay to leave the skin on—it adds a fire-roasted flavor). Roughly chop the onion. Mix tomatoes, onion, and cilantro into the salsa. Taste and adjust seasoning as needed.

Ranchera Salsa

MAKES ABOUT 2 CUPS

Most salsas are best the day they are made, but this one tends to hold on to its flavor longer because of the dried chiles. It's not only awesome on carnitas tacos (page 116) and tamales (page 228), but on simple braised or grilled meats or chicken. Any leftovers make fantastic chilaquiles with homemade chips.

2 large vine-ripened tomatoes
2 jalapeño chiles, stems removed
8 dried chiles de árbol, stems removed
¼ small yellow onion
¼ cup cilantro leaves with stems
1 large garlic clove
1 teaspoon Diamond Crystal kosher salt
½ teaspoon cumin seed, toasted

In a 2- to 3-quart saucepan, place tomatoes and both fresh and dried chiles; add enough water to cover. Bring to a boil, then reduce heat and simmer until the dried chiles are soft and pliable, about 10 minutes.

Drain tomatoes and chiles; cool slightly.

Remove the tomato skins; they will slip off easily in one soft pinching motion. Place tomatoes, chiles, and all remaining ingredients in a blender and purée until smooth. *(Can be made 3 days ahead. Cover and refrigerate.)*

KITCHEN NOTE: Use the leftover salsa and chips to make chilaquiles for breakfast in the a.m. You're welcome!

Avocado & Purple Tomatillo Salsa

MAKES ABOUT 1 CUP (RECIPE DOUBLES EASILY)

Spice can vary with jalapeños, so if you like a nice kick, look for chiles with dark wrinkles or lines on them—those will increase the heat level. Wild purple tomatillos are smaller and have a sweeter flavor than their green counterpart, and let me tell you, plant them once and you'll have them in your garden forever! The lovely lantern-laden branches also give lushness to summer flower arrangements.

1½ teaspoons Diamond Crystal kosher salt, divided
1 large jalapeño chile
8 to 10 purple tomatillos or 3 large green tomatillos, husks removed
1 avocado, quartered
½ cup (packed) cilantro leaves with stems
¼ cup water
1 large garlic clove
1 teaspoon fresh lime juice (from 1 lime)

Bring a large pot of water to a boil with ½ teaspoon salt. Using a paring knife, pierce the side of the jalapeño. Add the jalapeño and tomatillos to the water and boil until tomatillos turn a slightly yellowish color and soften, about 15 minutes. Using a slotted spoon, remove the tomatillos and jalapeño.

Cut the stem off the jalapeño and discard. Add the tomatillos, jalapeño, avocado, cilantro, water, garlic, lime juice, and remaining 1 teaspoon salt to a blender and purée until smooth. Taste for seasoning. *(Can be made 2 days ahead. Cover and refrigerate.)*

Green Olive Lemon Relish

MAKES ABOUT ⅓ CUP

This is equally good as a condiment on grilled fish or chicken.

¼ cup chopped pitted Castelvetrano green olives
2 tablespoons extra-virgin olive oil
2 tablespoons finely chopped Meyer lemon (peel and all, but no seeds; from 1 lemon)
12 oregano leaves, torn
¼ teaspoon freshly grated garlic
Flaky sea salt
Cayenne pepper

Mix olives, oil, lemon, oregano, and garlic in a bowl. Season with a pinch of salt and cayenne. *(Can be made 1 day ahead. Cover and refrigerate.)*

SAUCES

Chimichurri Sauce

MAKES ABOUT 1¼ CUPS

A wonderful accompaniment to any grilled protein or such simply prepared veggies as eggplant, zucchini, and potatoes.

½ cup extra-virgin olive oil
½ cup finely chopped cilantro with stems
¼ cup finely chopped Italian parsley
¼ cup sherry vinegar
2 green onions (white parts only), finely chopped
2 garlic cloves, minced
2 tablespoons finely chopped fresh oregano
1 teaspoon flaky sea salt
½ teaspoon dried red chile flakes

Mix all ingredients in a medium bowl. *(Can be made 1 day ahead. Cover and refrigerate; stir before serving.)*

Homemade Barbecue Sauce

MAKES ABOUT 1½ CUPS

I rarely buy barbecue sauce because I typically have all of the ingredients to make a delicious homemade version in my refrigerator and pantry.

¼ cup ketchup
¼ cup honey
¼ cup Dijon mustard
3 tablespoons Sriracha hot sauce
3 tablespoons low-sodium soy sauce
3 tablespoons unsulphured molasses
3 tablespoons raw apple cider vinegar
1 teaspoon smoked paprika
Diamond Crystal kosher salt and freshly ground pepper

Mix ketchup, honey, mustard, Sriracha, soy sauce, molasses, vinegar, and paprika in a bowl, whisking until smooth. Season with salt and pepper. (*Can be made 5 days ahead. Cover and refrigerate.*)

Tahini Yogurt Sauce

MAKES ABOUT 1 CUP

This sauce is great drizzled on fritters, as a dip for crudités, on Grilled Purple Sprouting Broccoli (page 186), or to pair with Chicken with Smoked Paprika (page 179) or Moroccan Lamb Meatballs (page 155).

⅓ cup extra-virgin olive oil
¼ cup fresh lemon juice (from 1 large lemon)
3 tablespoons plain Greek yogurt (full fat)
2 tablespoons tahini
1 garlic clove, finely grated
1 teaspoon Diamond Crystal kosher salt
¼ teaspoon Piment d'Espelette or Aleppo pepper (see Spice Drawer, page 274)

Whisk all ingredients in a bowl to blend. (*Can be made 3 days ahead; cover and refrigerate.*)

Aioli

MAKES ABOUT 2/3 CUP

When making aioli, my saving grace was the discovery of that magical plastic insert tube in the food processor. You still have to add the oil very slowly in the beginning, but just about when your shoulder starts to ache, the aioli will begin to come together—and that's when, voilà!, you pour the remaining oil through the insert-lined tube and let the slow, consistent drizzle be your helper.

1 egg
1 egg yolk
1 teaspoon Dijon mustard
2 large garlic cloves, grated
1 tablespoon fresh lemon juice (from ½ lemon)
1½ teaspoons flaky sea salt
½ cup safflower or grapeseed oil
½ cup extra-virgin olive oil
1 to 2 teaspoons water (optional)

In a food processor, emulsify the egg, yolk, mustard, garlic, lemon juice, and sea salt until completely incorporated. Mix the two oils together in a measuring cup with a spout, and very slowly (beginning with droplets) and with the processor running, add the oil through the feed tube. This should take several minutes. Once half of the oil has been added by drops, begin adding the remaining oil in a very thin, slow, steady stream, about 1 teaspoon at a time. Once the mayonnaise comes together, you can add the rest of the oil a little more liberally, but continue to do so through the tube. At the end, add water to thin the aioli if it's too thick. (*Can be made 2 days ahead. Cover and refrigerate.*)

Heirloom Tomato Sauce

MAKES ABOUT 4 CUPS

This summer sauce makes great use of those awkward-ly shaped, semi-bruised heirloom tomatoes that are difficult to slice but oh so delicious. The anchovies add a savory, salty flavor that's not fishy, I promise. Grating the tomatoes is a technique I learned almost ten years ago in a Moroccan cooking class taught by my friend Peggy Markel, who leads culinary tours of Morocco and Italy. It's a magical technique that saves time—no peeling! As for the Calabrian chiles, they have wonder-ful flavor and heat that really make the sauce delec-table; look for them in jars packed in oil at specialty Italian markets.

2½ pounds cluster or heirloom tomatoes or a mix of
    garden tomatoes
4 anchovies packed in oil, drained
3 tablespoons extra-virgin olive oil
4 large garlic cloves, grated
2 small oil-packed Calabrian chiles, stemmed, chopped
    or ½ teaspoon dried red chile flakes
2 teaspoons Diamond Crystal kosher salt
6 tablespoons (¾ stick) chilled unsalted butter, cut into
    pieces

Using the large-holed side of a box grater, hold the tomato by its stem end and grate until you are left only with the skins (give them to your chickens or use to flavor vegetable broth).

In a large skillet on medium-high heat, fry the ancho-vies in olive oil, mashing the fillets with a wooden spoon until they resemble a paste, about 1 minute. Next add the garlic and chiles, and cook until fragrant, about 1 minute (it will smell ahh-mazing!). Now add the tomatoes and salt, and cook, stirring occasionally, until the sauce reduces some of its wateriness, 15 to 20 minutes. Remove from heat, add the butter, and stir just until melted. *(Can be made 2 days ahead. Cool, then cover and refrigerate.)*

CHIPS, CROUTONS & TORTILLAS

Swiss Chard Chips

4 SERVINGS

You can make chips from virtually any greens you have in your crisper or garden, and I learned early on that it's the easiest way to get veggies into my kids' diet. Turning down the heat on these greens chips allows them to hold on to their nutrition without losing any crispness.

Feel free to look beyond chard, too. Beets and kohlrabi are an economical option—you get two veggies (the root and the attached leafy greens) for the price of one. I always buy veggies with the greens attached because I can see how fresh the produce is. If the greens are crisp and lush looking, then the bulb will taste fresh.

12 Swiss chard, kale stalks, or leafy tops from 1 bunch
    kohlrabi or beets
1 tablespoon grapeseed oil
1 teaspoon sesame seeds (optional)
½ teaspoon flaky sea salt

Preheat the oven to 200°F. Line a large baking sheet with parchment paper. Strip leaves off the chard and tear the larger pieces in half. Toss chard, oil, seeds, and salt on the baking sheet, spreading leaves out in a single layer. Bake leaves until dry and crisp, about 18 to 20 minutes. Cool completely. *(Can be made 2 days ahead. Store in an airtight container at room tem-perature.)*

Herb Croutons

MAKES 2 CUPS

Tearing the bread into irregular pieces gives the croutons a nice rustic appeal. These are great sprinkled over your favorite soup or salad.

6 tablespoons extra-virgin olive oil
2 heaping teaspoons fresh thyme leaves
2 cups torn baguette pieces (from 1 baguette)
Diamond Crystal kosher salt
2 garlic cloves, minced

Heat oil in a large skillet over medium-high heat. Add the thyme and cook until it starts to perfume your kitchen—it might pop and splatter a bit. Next, add the baguette pieces and season with salt. Toss the bread in the oil until coated. Sauté until crispy and brown, about 5 minutes. Add the garlic at the very end and cook for about 1 minute. Taste for seasoning. Place croutons in a bowl lined with paper towels and let stand until ready to use. *(Croutons can be made 1 day ahead.)*

Homemade Tortillas

MAKES ABOUT 15 SMALL TORTILLAS

Tortillas are so fun to make. But if you're short on time, don't feel guilty—seek out good tortillas from a Mexican grocery or restaurant. If a supermarket is your only option, choose Guerrero or La Banderita Ricas corn tortillas, which I find to be the most tender and tasty of the packaged options.

2 cups Bob's Red Mill masa harina
½ teaspoon flaky sea salt
1½ cups warm water
1 teaspoon fresh lime juice (from 1 lime)

Combine masa harina (corn flour) and salt in a large bowl; add water and lime juice, and mix with your hands until combined (this is part of the fun—just do it). If the dough seems a little dry, add more warm water (it's all about feel; the dough should hold together and look like Play-Doh). Cover with a dish towel and let rest 20 minutes at room temperature.

One at a time, shape the dough into Ping-Pong–size balls; press flat on a tortilla press between two pieces of plastic or parchment paper. Alternatively, you can place dough between the parchment and roll out with a rolling pin.

Heat a griddle or large heavy skillet over medium-high heat. Working in batches, add tortillas and cook for 2 minutes. Flip and cook for an additional 30 seconds (my tortilla press makes tortillas that are on the thicker side, so you might find that your tortillas cook a little more quickly).

Wrap the warm tortillas in a dish towel and place the whole wrapped package in a gallon-size Ziplock bag until you are ready to eat or up to 20 minutes before serving. Don't open the bag until mealtime and they will stay nice and toasty.

Cherry Tomato & Gin Jam

MAKES ABOUT 1 CUP

This is a fantastic spread on sprouted sourdough bread loaded with aged goat cheese and arugula, or over Moroccan Lamb Meatballs in Lettuce Cups (see page 155). It'll also take that end-of-summer burger up a notch.

1 tablespoon extra-virgin olive oil

1 tablespoon butter

3 tablespoons minced shallot (about 1 large shallot)

1 pint (2 cups) cherry tomatoes

⅓ cup gin

2 tablespoons (packed) brown sugar

1 teaspoon Diamond Crystal kosher salt

¼ teaspoon dried red chile flakes

1 tablespoon red wine vinegar

1 teaspoon coarsely chopped fresh oregano leaves (or oregano flowers)

Heat oil and butter in a heavy medium saucepan over medium-high heat. Once it foams, add shallot, then reduce heat to medium. Add tomatoes and sauté for 3 to 5 minutes. As the tomatoes start to break down, add gin, sugar, salt, and chile flakes. Cook until sauce begins to thicken, pushing down the tomatoes with a wooden spoon to smash, about 10 minutes. Mix in vinegar and oregano, and cook for 1 minute. Cool completely. (*Jam can be made 1 week ahead. Cover and refrigerate. Bring to room temperature before using.*)

Apricot Jam with Lemon Verbena

MAKES ABOUT 1½ CUPS

In the early '60s, my father flew to Belgium to ask my mom's parents for her hand in marriage. When he landed in rainy Brussels, he was totally wiped after days of travel. Luckily, he was picked up from the airport by a dear family friend, Gill Van den Broeck, who quickly put him to bed on a sofa in her apartment. He awoke from his nap to a plate of fragrant, fluffy Belgian waffles stuffed with apricot jam. A "Welcome to Belgium" doesn't get better than that! My dad talks about it to this day, and my mom still serves waffles with apricot jam.

I wait all year for our Blenheim apricot tree to fruit, and I even load up on extras at the farmers market. The fruit is small in size but not in flavor. By the end of the week, it's rare that any apricots will be left in the fruit bowl, so this small batch of jam is a nice way to keep apricot season alive in your fridge! If you can find it, lemon verbena goes so beautifully with apricots—but the jam is delicious with or without it.

1½ pounds apricots (about 8 to 10 apricots), pitted, sliced

1 cup sugar

¼ cup fresh lemon juice or more if needed (from 1 large lemon)

1 sprig fresh lemon verbena

Combine apricots, sugar, and lemon juice in a heavy medium saucepan over medium heat. Bring to simmer, stirring occasionally. Continue to simmer until jam begins to thicken, about 15 minutes, stirring occasionally and taking care to skim off any of the foam that rises to the top. Taste, adding more lemon juice if needed. Continue to cook 2 minutes longer. Add lemon verbena; remove pan from heat. Let rest in the pan an additional 5 to 10 minutes. Discard lemon verbena. Pour jam into a clean jar and seal. (*Can be made 3 weeks ahead. Refrigerate.*)

Blackberry & Mulberry Jam

MAKES ABOUT 2½ CUPS

We have a 100-year-old mulberry tree in our backyard that bears the most delicious blackberry-esque fruit. The fruit appears all at once, so it's a mad dash to collect it all before the bugs and birds attack. Simultaneously, blackberry brambles are in full tilt. If you don't happen to have such "problems," substitute with whatever mixture of berries you have—raspberries or blackberries work well. We find the best way to enjoy the fruit is to cook it simply until the juices are just released, and then pour the mixture over an open biscuit or waffle (page 134).

1½ pounds mixed berries, such as mulberries and
    blackberries, divided
1½ cups sugar
6 tablespoons fresh Meyer lemon juice (from 2 lemons)

Pour all but 1 cup of berries into a pot with the sugar and lemon juice. Simmer until jam begins to thicken, stirring occasionally and skimming any foam that rises to the top (scoop foam into a small bowl*), about 30 minutes. Add the reserved berries and continue to cook an additional 5 minutes. Turn off the heat and let rest in the pan for an additional 5 to 10 minutes. Pour jam into clean jars and seal. *(Can be made 3 weeks ahead. Refrigerate.)*

* Jam Syrup: Your little bowl of foam will settle down into a nice little syrup. Strain it through a fine strainer to remove any seeds and store in the fridge for up to 2 weeks. Note that it makes for a lovely summer spritzer when combined with a sparkling cava (see Bar Tips & Tools, page 283).

Preserved Meyer Lemons

MAKES 2 PINTS

In the early summer, I still have tons of Meyer lemons on our trees that I need to use before the next setting of fruit occurs. Simultaneously, all those pots I over-ambitiously filled with herbs are flowering. So I make this and use it as a simple, wonderful condiment that's chopped into chicken, fish, salads, tartines, or sauces.

¼ cup Diamond Crystal kosher salt
3 Meyer lemons, cut lengthwise into quarters
6 flowering oregano sprigs
½ teaspoon whole coriander seed
2 chiles de árbol
2 pint jars with lids, sterile

Divide the ingredients between two jars, beginning with 1 tablespoon of salt in each, and start loading in the lemons with oregano, coriander, and chile until you can't fit any more lemon pieces. It's okay to squish the wedges; just don't smash them to oblivion—try to keep the integrity of the wedge shape. Add remaining salt and secure each lid. Turn upside down and store in a cool, dark place for 3 to 5 days. Check on the jars periodically, flipping the jars occasionally to move the liquid around the lemons. *(Can be made 6 months ahead. Store in a cool, dark place.)*

Quick Pickles

MAKES 1 TO 2 CUPS (DEPENDING ON VEGGIES USED)

This is my go-to pickle when I'm in a pinch and need a bright-tasting note to pop on the plate. I use it for persimmons, beets, cucumbers, and chiles. While you can combine other vegetables, keep beets on their own because they'll color everything a bright magenta. This recipe is simple, easy, and very versatile.

2 cups unseasoned rice vinegar
½ cup sugar
2 teaspoons coriander seeds
2 teaspoons Diamond Crystal kosher salt
2 Fuyu persimmons, beets, or Persian cucumbers or 4 jalapeños, thinly sliced

Mix the vinegar, sugar, coriander, and salt in a large, sterile jar until dissolved. Add the sliced fruit or vegetables and let stand at least 30 minutes. *(Can be made 3 weeks ahead. Cover and refrigerate.)*

Moroccan Bread & Butter Zucchini Pickles

MAKES 4 PINTS

With great crunch and zippy flavor, these remind me of the zucchini pickles we've loved at Zuni Cafe in San Francisco. The Moroccan spices make the marinade delicious with so many of the veggies in my summer harvest basket; try using it with shishito peppers, bush or pole beans, or lemon cucumber. I use a hand mandoline to slice all of the veggies so they're the same thickness. These pickles are a welcome addition to a mezze board, burger, or sandwich.

2 pounds zucchini
1 sweet onion
1 large jalapeño or 2 fresno chile peppers, stems removed, thinly sliced (seeds and all)

4 tablespoons salt, divided
2½ cups apple cider vinegar
1 cup raw or turbinado sugar
1 tablespoon yellow mustard seeds
2 teaspoons ras el hanout (see Spice Drawer, page 275)
1 teaspoon turmeric

Slice the zucchinis into ¼-inch rounds. Do the same with the onion. Toss the vegetables with 2 tablespoons salt and put in a large colander in the sink. The salt will help remove the excess water from the zucchini slices. Let sit for 20 minutes. In the meantime, place the vinegar, sugar, remaining salt, and spices in a small saucepan and cook, stirring, over medium heat until sugar and salt have dissolved. Dry the veggies well with clean kitchen towels and fit them into clean mason jars. Pour the warm mixture over the veggies and secure with a lid. *(Can be made 3 weeks ahead. Cover and refrigerate.)*

MORE ESSENTIALS

Spiced Rimming Salt

MAKES ABOUT ⅓ CUP

A cocktail with a salty, spiced rim adds an unbeatable flavor punch, and it's so easy to do! Pour the mixture onto a small plate to cover, then run a lime wedge around the rim of a glass, turn it upside down, and dip it into the salt. Great for a mezcal cocktail, a michelada, or a margarita, this also makes a fun hostess gift for a cocktail party.

¼ cup flaky sea salt
2 tablespoons plus 2 teaspoons Aleppo pepper (see Spice Drawer, page 274)
2 teaspoons turbinado sugar

Mix all ingredients and seal in a container. *(Can be made 1 month ahead. Store at room temperature.)*

No-Stir Chicken Stock

MAKES ABOUT 8 TO 10 CUPS

Anytime I cook a whole chicken (see page 179), I reserve the bones and make stock the following day. This is a simple recipe, it costs less than store-bought stock, and the result blows the doors off of anything in a can or box.

1 tablespoon extra-virgin olive oil
Bones from a whole cooked chicken, any large bones cut in half
1 whole onion, cut into quarters
16 cups water
3 celery stalks with leaves, cut in half
2 carrots, cut in half
6 garlic cloves
8 parsley sprigs
2 tablespoons Diamond Crystal Kosher salt
2 fresh bay leaves
1 teaspoon whole black peppercorns

Heat oil in a large stockpot over high heat. Add chicken bones and onion, and cook until lightly browned, stirring often, about 10 minutes. Add water, celery, carrots, garlic, parsley, salt, bay leaves, and peppercorns. Simmer partially covered for 6 hours without stirring (if you stir it, it will get cloudy!). Strain stock. *(Can be made ahead. Cool, then cover and refrigerate up to 4 days or freeze up to 1 month.)*

Pâte Brisée

MAKES 2 DOUGH DISKS

This buttery pie crust is my go-to for pies, quiches, and galettes. It's easy to make with a quick buzz in the food processor, it bakes up crispy, and it holds its shape well—hence its use in the high-sided Quiche with Swiss Chard & Leek (see page 174).

2½ cups all-purpose flour
1 tablespoon sugar
1 teaspoon Diamond Crystal kosher salt
1 cup (2 sticks) unsalted butter, cut in small cubes, frozen
⅓ cup ice water

Add flour, sugar, and salt to a food processor fitted with a steel blade and pulse 5 times to incorporate. Add butter and pulse 5 times. Next, add water and pulse until a coarse meal forms. Divide mixture between two Ziplock plastic bags; using hands, squeeze until dough comes together. Press each into a disk. You'll see dime-size butter marks in the dough—they'll keep the crust flaky. Refrigerate at least 30 minutes. *(Can be made 3 days ahead and refrigerated or freeze up to 1 month. Soften at room temperature before rolling.)*

Honey & Maple Syrup Granola

MAKES ABOUT 2 QUARTS

When making homemade granola, I usually experiment with whatever nuts and dried fruits I have on hand in the pantry. I think this is one of my best renditions yet. At our house it's a favorite snack, or we have it for breakfast with a dollop of Greek yogurt. I also package it for gift-giving at the holidays or as a way to say thank you to friends.

2 cups old-fashioned oats (not instant)
1½ cups unsweetened, shredded large-flaked coconut
1 cup whole raw pecans
½ cup raw pepitas
½ cup raw pistachios or hazelnuts
6 tablespoons coconut oil, melted if solid
2 tablespoons honey
2 tablespoons pure maple syrup
1 teaspoon ground cinnamon

½ teaspoon flaky sea salt
1 cup unsweetened dried figs, cut in half
1 cup unsweetened dried cherries

Position rack in middle of oven and preheat to 325°F. Combine oats, coconut, pecans, pepitas, pistachios or hazelnuts, coconut oil, honey, syrup, cinnamon, and salt on a large rimmed baking sheet and toss well—I use my hands. Bake for 10 minutes. Using a metal spatula, stir to mix and continue baking until golden brown, about 10 minutes longer. Cool granola on the baking sheet, then mix in the dried fruit. Scoop ingredients into an airtight container and store in a cool place. It will keep a solid week—if it lasts that long!

Dried Persimmon Slices

MAKES 12 TO 16 CHIPS

The crunchiest variety of persimmon, Fuyus are great for making dried chips. I do have a fancy dehydrator with multiple racks, but I find the oven works just as well and is easier and quicker. Enjoy these on their own or as a garnish in your favorite cocktail.

2 Fuyu persimmons

Preheat the oven to 200°F. Line 2 baking sheets with parchment paper. Using a mandoline, thinly slice persimmons to yield a total of 12 to 16 slices. Arrange the slices in single layers on baking sheets. Bake until dry, turning persimmons over halfway through baking, about 2 hours. Cool completely. *(Can be made 1 week ahead. Store airtight at room temperature.)*

Dried Citrus Slices / Candied Citrus Slices

MAKES ABOUT 32 SLICES

Enjoy as a snack (you can eat the skin and all) or in your favorite cocktail. The candied ones are great as a garnish for cakes and cupcakes. You can string the oranges with pretty ribbon to make beautiful ornaments or gift toppers during the holidays.

4 firm seedless oranges or lemons
White sanding sugar (optional; for making Candied Citrus Slices*)

Preheat the oven to 200°F. Line 2 baking sheets with parchment paper. Using a mandoline, thinly slice oranges. Arrange the slices in single layers on baking sheets and bake until centers are dry, turning the sheet halfway through cooking, about 2 hours. Cool completely. *(Can be made 1 week ahead. Store airtight at room temperature.)*

* To make Candied Citrus Slices, add a sprinkling of sanding sugar to each slice just before baking.

Spice Drawer & Kitchen Tools

In these pages, I share my go-to spices, herbs, oils, and tools that I use on repeat—and I hope to inspire you to stock up on them, too.

SPICE DRAWER

One of the keys to creating delicious food is maintaining a well-stocked spice drawer. As you work your way through the recipes in this book, you'll see how the spices and herbs mentioned in this section are used frequently. I recommend purchasing all of them. It might feel like a big blow, but trust me, they will become mainstays in your kitchen. Most of the exotic spices can be found at Middle Eastern or Mexican markets (many are sold in bulk and are reasonably priced). For a variety of organic options, search online. I love buying large quantities and portioning them into jam jars to share with my friends and my mom.

Any number of herbs can be dried, and it's easier than you might think. Some, like rosemary, flowering cilantro or oregano, thyme, marjoram, lemon verbena, lavender, and sage, can be air dried. Tie the stems together with string and hang them upside down in an area that allows for plenty of air circulation. Most will dry completely in five to seven days.

High-moisture, herbaceous leaves like parsley, cilantro, oregano, marjoram, mint, dill, and tarragon can also be dried in an oven. Separate the leaves from the stems and place in a single layer on a baking sheet. Bake at the lowest temperature until dry, checking for doneness after 1 hour. Once they have dried and cooled, store herbs in jars with tight-fitting lids. Similarly, you can dry herbs quickly in the microwave. Simply detach the leaves from the stems and place on a microwave-safe dish, then zap on high for 2 to 3 minutes.

ALEPPO PEPPER
Named for Aleppo, a town in northern Syria, the semi-dried burgundy-colored Halaby chile peppers are dried and then crushed or coarsely ground. Their moderate heat level adds a ton of flavor—a little spicy, a bit sweet, and a tad smoky. Sprinkle on roasted meats, fish, shellfish, vegetables, salads, eggs, pasta, or cheese. Available at Middle Eastern markets, some specialty foods stores, and online.

ANCHO CHILE
Dried, whole-roasted, ripened poblano peppers are a deep reddish brown and sweet with mild heat. Available at Mexican markets and most supermarkets.

CHILE DE ÁRBOL
This small, thin, spicy, dried Mexican pepper is about two to three inches long and has a smoky, grassy flavor. Also known as a bird's beak chile, it's comparable in heat to a serrano and maintains its beautiful red color when dried. Available at Mexican markets and many supermarkets.

FENNEL POLLEN
Wild fennel grows predominately in Italy and California. The pollen is harvested by hand, which makes it special and, also, kinda pricey. It has aromatic flavors of licorice and citrus.

GUAJILLO CHILE
The dried form of the Mexican mirasol chile, the guajillo has a thick skin and flavor notes of green tea and berries. There are two main varieties; the other is the guajillo puya chile, which is smaller (about four inches long) and hotter, with a crimson color. Available at Mexican markets and many supermarkets.

HIBISCUS, DRIED
Also known as Flor de Jamaica, the dried flowers are typically steeped in boiling water to make agua de jamaica. It has a deep red color when reconstituted and is tart and refreshing. Available at Mexican markets and many supermarkets.

PEPPERCORNS, PINK
The dried berry of the Peruvian pepper tree is bright pink, fragrant, and slightly floral with citrus notes. Great sprinkled over meats or cheese. Available at specialty foods stores and online.

PIMENT D'ESPELETTE
This French pepper from the Pyrenees region is used in Basque cooking. It's finely ground and is my preference for even distribution of seasoning, with a heat range between cayenne and Aleppo peppers. Available at specialty foods stores and online.

RAS EL HANOUT
Ras el hanout is a fragrant and beautiful North African blend of spices that often includes coriander, turmeric, clove, chile peppers, cinnamon, and cumin. In Arabic, ras el hanout means "head of the shop," so it's literally the best offering at the spice shop. Every shop carries its own unique blend, and I've never tried one I didn't love. Once you taste it, you'll try to figure out other ways to incorporate it in your cooking repertoire. Available at specialty foods stores and online.

SMOKED PAPRIKA
Made from pimiento peppers that have been dried and smoked over oak, then ground. It is sold sweet and mild (dulce), medium hot (agridulce), and hot (picante). Available at specialty foods stores and many supermarkets.

SUMAC
Sumac is a tangy, lemony spice often used in Mediterranean and Middle Eastern cooking. Available at Middle Eastern markets, specialty foods stores, and online.

ZA'ATAR
Za'atar is a Middle Eastern spice blend of dried thyme, oregano, marjoram, sesame seeds, salt, and occasionally sumac. Available at Middle Eastern markets, specialty foods stores, and online.

SALT & PEPPER TALK

BLACK PEPPER
Please, please, always grind pepper yourself. Store-bought ground pepper lacks the intense flavor of freshly ground. In recipes where cracked pepper is called for, you'll want to adjust the grinder for a coarser grind. There's one exception, and a confession—I do buy pre-ground white pepper. The flavor is more delicate, and a pinch goes a long way. It's often used in white sauces or other dishes where a peppery note is needed but you don't want black pepper flecks.

DIAMOND CRYSTAL KOSHER SALT
I call for this brand in most of my cooking, as it has a light, clean, fresh taste and no additives. Most importantly, it has fifty-three percent less sodium compared with regular table salt. A warning: If you use a different salt, please cut the amount in half to avoid over salting. Available at specialty foods stores, some supermarkets, and online.

FLAKY SEA SALT
Large, thin, crunchy, delicate sea salt flakes are typically used as a finishing salt to sprinkle over dishes just before serving to brighten flavors. My favorite brands are Maldon and Jacobsen. Available at specialty foods stores, most supermarkets, and online.

A LITTLE BIT ON OLIVE OIL

When our oldest daughter, Ava, was a baby, we rented an apartment in Florence for the fall. My lack of Italian didn't stop me from venturing out onto the cobblestone streets and making my best attempt to communicate. My cheeks flush with embarrassment remembering myself at the Mercato Centrale, trying to articulate to a very handsome butcher what cut of meat I needed. What I lacked in language I eventually developed in palate, especially in regard to olive oil. Oh, the olive oil was so amazing. Italians are not scared of olive oil, not one bit, no ma'am. New oil is like the Italian version of ketchup, and it goes on everything from plain bread to soups to beef. And then there are the olive oil shots in the morning! Tuscan oil in particular is out of this world—peppery and zippy and strong. I've been hooked ever since, and the Tuscan oil offered seasonally online at the Rare Wine Company is bellissimo.

Olive oil turns bad quickly, so if you pick up a good one or are gifted a nice bottle, make sure to use it within three months.

KITCHEN TOOLS

Here are a few things I use constantly, regardless of the season:

CAZUELA
This terracotta Spanish cooking pot cooks things so beautifully! And what's more garden-to-table than cooking in terracotta? Works on the stovetop or in the oven, and cooks everything—savory or sweet. Everything always turns out moist and delicious. You can find good ones at tienda.com.

DISH TOWELS
Seems ordinary, but we use dish towels for so many kitchen tasks. I love a classic 100% cotton tea towel or even flour sacks. They absorb well and don't leave lint on your dishes.

IMMERSION BLENDER
Easy to clean and purées beautifully. We use it for soups, sauces, and juicing fruit. It's handy for the bar, too.

INSTANT-READ THERMOMETER
Not just for meat but for dessert, too! Truly essential.

JUICER
I have the most amazingly fun and effective juicer from Breville. Its pull-down mechanism makes grapefruits a breeze to squeeze. Fresh-squeezed juice will stay good in the refrigerator for up to three days, but it's the very best on day one.

MICROPLANE OR HANDHELD RASP
I don't care what the brand is, but I use one! Great for grating myriad foods, from garlic to citrus zest to nutmeg.

MINI ANGLED MEASURING CUP (OXO)
Get one designated metal measuring cup with ounces and tablespoons for your bar and another for your kitchen. This cup makes measuring for salad dressings and cocktails a cinch.

Garden Shed

THE GLORY OF GARDENING: HANDS IN THE DIRT, HEAD IN THE SUN, HEART WITH NATURE.
TO NURTURE A GARDEN IS TO FEED NOT JUST ON THE BODY, BUT THE SOUL.
— ALFRED AUSTIN

My garden in Santa Barbara sits in the zone hardiness of 10a, which basically means we get a lot of sun exposure and the ground never freezes. Our climate in Southern California mimics that of the Mediterranean, so we're able to grow many of the same fruits and vegetables, and the Mediterranean style of cooking suits our products. My garden is equipped with four four-by-eight-by-eighteen-inch vegetable beds, all of which host a revolving door of produce. Beyond the beds, I plant directly in the earth, in large terracotta pots, and in wine crates (we always seem to have these on hand…hmm). I apparently have a serious gardening problem, because even though I'm short on space, I just can't stop planting. If you find a support group for my type of issue, please let me know.

Santa Barbara's soil tends to be clay packed (this is, after all, the land of the adobe), so when we plant directly in the ground, we amend the soil with a mixture of sand, compost, and an amendment containing bat guano and worm castings (from G&B Organics from Kellogg). When this works, it's awesome, but sometimes this type of planting sets up a direct competition with critters, and sometimes I feel like I'm channeling Bill Murray in *Caddyshack*. An easy fix for deterring critters (no, not dynamite) is using wire cloches or shaping chicken wire into rounds and fixing them to the earth with ground staples. This helps prevent plants from getting eaten by the rabbits, chipmunks, birds, and squirrels in our yard. In the beds we use the same technique for protecting dainty leafy greens and newly sown seeds.

We don't have an orchard per se, but our yard is interspersed with fruit-bearing trees. They grow well right in the soil, and some thrive in large terracotta pots. I love the sculptural way a potted fruit tree punctuates a garden—it makes an aesthetic statement and (bonus!) feeds us.

We also host a bee box in the garden, and I plant with the bees in mind, often adding in flowers for easier pollination. That system (fingers crossed) leads to a better yield of produce, healthier bees, and a thriving hive.

I often plant succulents and herbs together because they both have the same watering needs, or hydrozones (see photo, page 173). Many herbs are drought tolerant, and many herbs are perennials, so they make great borders with less water needs. Sculptural succulents mixed with lacy herbs are so stunningly and archetypally "Santa Barbara."

When we moved into our home, there was the framework for a formal rose garden but no plants—a blank canvas that was a gift from the garden gods. I got right to work, planting my favorite rose varieties and dahlias along with a border of hellebores interspersed with chocolate-scented geraniums, which add a lushness in off seasons (especially in January when we prune the roses). I also planted such seasonal bulbs as tulips, iris, and ranunculus, so we have flowers popping up for year-round cutting. Because of our climate zone, I rarely dig up bulbs for storage—I can just leave them in the earth for the next season.

GARDEN TOOLS

For storage, we built a potting table complete with a vintage sink that transforms on warm nights into the perfect lush-life, self-serve bar. Also in the bar, I mean potting bench, I have a few tools that get regular use.

BAMBOO STAKES
Handy to support peppers, eggplants, dahlias, and bush beans so they don't flop on the ground.

COMPOST
We make compost in a four-foot-square frame fitted with chicken wire. It sits in an area that gets full sun but is hidden from the main traffic areas. The chickens eat many of our vegetable scraps, but we use their "scraps" in the compost, along with brown garden cuttings, newspaper, eggshells, and coffee grinds. I don't add citrus because it doesn't break down well and the acidity kills the worms and beneficial biomatter.

GARDEN JOURNAL & PENCIL
Great for keeping track of planting and harvest dates, as well as notes about what's growing well and what's not. And for me as a busy mom, it's a place to jot down completely random things I've forgotten as they pop into my head. Fun fact: The pencil doubles as a planting tool—the shaved area at the point is the perfect size for making holes for seeds.

GARDEN STAPLES
These large, U-shaped metal pieces fix wire cloches or trellising cages to the soil so they won't topple over.

JAPANESE PLANTING KNIFE
Makes me feel like I'm a samurai in a Kurosawa movie, and it really makes planting easy. The edges of the knife create tidy lines in the soil for sowing seeds, and the point is great for digging the holes for transplanting seedlings.

LATEX-FREE GLOVES
Sounds a little creepy, doesn't it? But honestly, I use these dishwashing gloves for the garden because they're thin, long (covering up to my upper forearm), and snug fitting—plus, they allow you to feel the earth better than heavier gloves. Sometimes garden gloves get dried and crunchy, but these guys wash up easily.

MULCH
I use Kellogg's Harvest Supreme—it's full of beneficial organic matter and is the right consistency to make a nice blanket. It's the Goldilocks of mulch: not too fine and not too coarse.

ORGANIC FERTILIZER
Plant fertilizers are determined by their percentage of nitrogen, phosphorus, and potassium (N-P-K). They help boost the development and well-being of the seedling or plant. The lower percentages (under ten percent) indicate an organic product, so pick one with low numbers (like four-six-two, or basically any ratio under ten). My rule of thumb is to add fertilizer first when you plant and again when the plants flower.

RAFFIA WIRE TIES
I'm not crazy about plastic in the garden, so those kelly-green plastic ties are not my favorite. Raffia-covered wire is natural looking and holds plants and tendrils in place when they get wayward and wonky.

SMALL PRUNERS
I have a bunch of inexpensive pruners because I don't treat my tools well enough to justify Felcos—I've learned that the hard way. I keep one in my kitchen for potted herbs, one in my garage for flower arranging, one in the rose garden, and one at my potting bench.

WIRE CLOCHES
I use these to protect newly sowed areas or young seedlings from wildlife. I like the ones sold on gardeners.com.

GARDEN TIPS

My criteria for selecting plants are to choose fruits and veggies that not only grow well in our climate but are unusual varieties that you can't easily find at the grocery store. For lists of what to plant when, check out the introductions to each of the season chapters (pages 19, 83, 139, and 199). I use each season's equinox as my cue to plant for the next season: late March for summer, late June for fall, late September for winter, and late December for spring.

For planting success, healthy soil is your most valued investment. You'll want to pick up the best-quality organic potting soil possible, something rich in friendly microbes like mycorrhizae. An organic mulch of a fine to medium weight should also be on your list because it helps keep weeds at bay and maintains a healthy, moist, and nutrient-rich soil.

I think it's best to start a garden with seedlings (or transplants) over seeds because seeds are most successfully propagated in a greenhouse where the temperature is controlled and birds are denied access. Seedlings are sold in packs of six, or individually in four-by-four-inch containers, and can be easily plugged into your soil. There's insurance in planting in multiples (six or more), especially if it's something you're really excited about, because not all seedlings will make it.

In general, vegetables and herbs need more than six hours per day of full sun. Wherever you plant, even if it's just a few terracotta pots on your patio, watch out for sun-blocking barriers and, if possible, plant near a water source so you don't have to drag around a watering can every time your plants need a drink.

If a big commitment scares you and/or space is tight, you can start out with large terracotta pots drilled with holes for drainage. If you're ready for more, hit the nursery for a kit you can assemble with the help of a friend. The best planting beds are the tallest: eighteen inches high (or more) to deter rabbits, accommodate root systems, and save your back. A raised bed also gives you better control of soil nutrients (the more nutrient-dense the soil, the more nutritious the veggies) and moisture levels. Beds should be lined with gopher wire and sprinkled with perlite (which helps break down clay-laden soil). Fill with a combination of your own garden dirt, finished organic compost, soil amendment, and organic potting soil. After constantly schlepping trellises and tomato cages in and out of my beds, I decided to fix frames of two-by-fours (see photo on page 280) for easy trellising in any season. We drill holes into the sides of these lumber frames so we can string garden twine for easy trellising.

When it's time to plant, dig holes wide enough to fit the root ball in the prepared bed, following tag instructions and guidelines for space; remove plants from the container by squeezing the plastic to loosen and hold the stem, gently turn upside down, and use gravity to tease them out. Loosen any impacted roots on the bottom of the root ball and place the plants into the holes, moving the soil around the base to snuggle it in, and then give it a good watering.

Any time I plant something new, I add a little organic fertilizer to give the new plant a little boost. Think of it as a shot of espresso first thing in the morning. Fertilizers have different directions, so just follow the instructions on the container.

Don't forget to secure the plant tag so you don't forget what you planted, or you might get your spicy peppers mixed with the sweet. Trust me, I know from experience.

Next, add a two-to-three-inch blanket of mulch. This is especially important in the hot summer months because it helps seal in moisture so you don't have to water as frequently. If you have a good coverage of mulch, you'll only need to water once or twice a week. The mulch also helps keep weeds at bay and has the added bonus of making the beds look tidy.

Set a date two times a week to water and check on the critters and your plants' watering needs. I actually write these dates in my appointment calendar. Before you water, dig down a few inches—if the soil is damp to the touch, you don't need to water. Overwatering dilutes the flavor of your vegetables.

Bar Tips & Tools

Below are my recommendations for stocking your own bar. They make up a variety of price points and styles of spirits and wines. Adjust to your own taste, but consider taking a risk and trying something new to add to your collection. The wine recommendations are what we consider our "house" wines.

Organize your bar for easy usage—keep spirits near their common pairings. So Cointreau should be nestled near its darling tequila (see the margaritas on pages 25, 91, 144, 145, and 205). Same goes for the vermouth, Campari, and gin (see the negronis on 146).

I also like to keep after-dinner options on hand: tawny port, Madeira, Amaro, or Scotch...or you can always return to Champagne. If you can spare the room in your fridge, always have a bottle of Champagne chilling—you never know who might stop by.

APERITIFS
Lillet Blanc, Oloroso sherry, St. Germain elderflower, Suze gentian, Benedictine, Campari, St. George Bruto Americano

BEER
Victoria pilsner, IPA, Belgian ale

BITTERS
Cocktail bitters are spirits typically infused with herbs, fruits, and spices. Favorites include Aztec chocolate bitters (with cinnamon and chile flavors; great with a black manhattan), old-fashioned bitters (Fee Brothers have clove notes, which is why they get a lot of play around the holidays), and Angostura bitters (also considered old-fashioned bitters, but the base is made with alcohol and has spice and citrus notes).

BRANDY
Calvados, St. George pear brandy, Pisco Portón, Pisco Campo de Encanto

CHAMPAGNE
Don't get hung up on vintages for Champagne. Even in off years, most quality producers still produce great wine; if it's not up to par, they won't release it. A non-vintage is a blend of vintages of a few years and is offered a few times each decade. Favorite producers include Chartogne-Taillet, Savart, Jérôme Prévost, Benoit Lahaye, and Benoit Marguet. See also On Champagne, page 209.

DIGESTIF
Amaro Averna (a bitter Italian variety made with a secret blend of herbs, spices, roots, and citrus)

GIN
It's no secret to anyone who knows me that gin is my favorite spirit. Most gin starts out as the same neutral grain alcohol, and then juniper and natural botanicals are added. The timing and emphasis of when and which botanicals are added make the difference in flavor, viscosity, and style. While some gins have strong floral notes (those in the botanical style list below), others, like London dry varieties, are cleaner tasting because to be classified as "dry" they can't add botanicals after the final distillation.

Botanical Style: Bordiga Occitan (Italy), The Botanist (Scotland), Caorunn (Scotland), Hendrick's (Scotland), Gin Mare (Spain), or Monkey 47 (Germany)
London Dry: Fords, Brokers, No 3, Plymouth, or Beefeater
Others: Old Raj (made with saffron, this is viscous and 110 proof—you've been warned)

MADEIRA

The tangy brightness of Madeira makes it one of the favorite after-dinner drinks at our house. It's delicious with cheese and chocolate desserts, and it's an awesome addition to a bar because it is oxidized and keeps for a long time after opening. Try any of the offerings from the Rare Wine Company's Historic Series.

MEZCAL

Made from virtually any type of agave but not a specific type like its sister, tequila.
Vago Elote Espadin or Del Maguey Tobala (sip neat, please)

ORANGE LIQUEUR

I don't add agave or simple syrup to margaritas, I simply use good-quality orange liqueurs, which are plenty sweet. If you're looking for options other than Cointreau (our house standby), try Bols, Pierre Ferrand Dry Curaçao Orange, or Solerno Blood Orange.

PORTO

Unlike most red ports, the tawny and white ports can last after opening. *Tawny port:* Niepoort, Dows, Fonseca, or Graham's; white port: Sandeman Porto Apitiv Reserve

RUM

Lemon Hart & Son Original 1804, Gosling's Black Seal Bermuda, or Copalli White

SPARKLING WATER

Aqua de Piedra or Topo Chico (these have bigger bubbles than other brands, and bigger bubbles hold up when diluted with alcohol and mixers)

SPARKLING WINE

Raventós Cava, from Penedes, Spain (great for making spritzers)

SYRUP

Orgeat Syrup: An almond and orange flower syrup that's super handy to have in your bar. It's a delicious nonalcoholic sweetener excellent in coffee, or lemon or lime juice. You can make homemade versions or try Liquid Alchemist or Fee Brothers.

TEQUILA

Choose a quality tequila so you can serve it either simply or in a cocktail; try Maestro Dobel Diamonte (a lovely, smooth tequila that's moderately priced; great for ponche or just to sip neat), Codigo, Cava de Oro, Espolon, Tequila Ocho (blanco, reposado, anejo, extra anejo)

TONIC

Nowadays, almost every store has interesting tonic waters. Seek out something organic with natural ingredients. There's also tonic syrup from a few sources, which is a nice thing to have stocked in your bar—you can mix it with sparkling water.

VERMOUTH

Dolin de Chambery Dry (ideal for a classic martini with a lemon twist), Punt e Mes (from Piedmont; half-dry, half-sweet—perfect in negronis), Sacred English Spiced (small production with big taste)

VODKA

Koskenkorva (Finland, made from barley), Tito's (Texas, made from yellow corn), Chopin (Poland, made from potato), Sobieski (Poland, made from rye)

WHISKEY

Bourbon: Willett Pot Still Reserve, Eagle Rare, Hillrock Solera Aged, W.R. Weller
Rye: 1806 Hillrock Double-Cask, Sazerac, Whistle Pig 10 Year, Colonel E.H. Taylor Rye
Scotch: Springbank 15 Year Campbeltown single malt, Edradour 10 Year, Suntory Hibiki Japanese Harmony, Ichiro's Malt & Grain

BAR EXTRAS

Castelvetrano olives (or other whole green olives): Whatever you do, pick one in a simple salt brine, not in a marinade. A terrific green olive can turn a good martini great. These meaty Sicilian olives have a fresh, buttery texture and a sweet-smooth flavor. Any leftovers can be house marinated (page 210).

Luxardo Maraschino, Fabbri Amarena, or even Trader Joe's maraschino cherries: These sour cherries are candied and preserved in syrup. They are dense and chewy with a sweet-tart flavor. Leftover syrup is wonderful in homemade sodas or desserts.

Sea salts: Use good-quality flaky sea salt or Spiced Rimming Salt (page 271) as an instant upgrade to any cocktail. Keep salts in an airtight container wide enough to fit the rim of a glass so you're not running all over looking for the rimming salt when you could be relaxing over a cocktail.

BAR TOOLS

These are the tools in my bar that I use regularly. I prefer my martinis stirred and my margaritas shaken; just make sure to hold the lid tight on the shaker—the last thing you want to do is fling blood orange juice all over your kitchen and clothes.

BARWARE
Nick and Nora: 4 ounces
Cocktail coupe: 5 to 7 ounces
Double old-fashioned: 12 to 16 ounces
Rocks glass: 6 to 8 ounces
Collins glass: 14 ounces

COCKTAIL SHAKER WITH STRAINER TOP
Get the largest one possible so you can fit large-batch drinks.

DOUBLE-HINGED CORKSCREW
You will never see a sommelier without one of these small, durable, and inexpensive corkscrews. The hinge mechanism helps pull the cork in a straight, vertical line so it comes out easily. It can be found at just about any wine shop or online.

DOUBLE ICE BUCKET

Handy to have on hand for parties and big enough to chill down two bottles at once. Handy especially in the summer if you are drinking a white and a light-bodied red that should be kept chilled.

FUN ICE

Love your home ice program—you can make your own with molds, or a lot of specialty grocery stores are now offering "fancy ice." Try the Williams Sonoma King Cube Tray with Lid, or see the Resource Guide (page 289) for bulk ice.

ICE SCOOP

Don't waste your time with ice tongs. Get a grip with a good designated scoop for filling glassware and cocktail shakers.

IMMERSION BLENDER

Awesome for quickly muddling—just a few pulses (see Strawberry Mezcal Margaritas, page 91)—or puréeing whole fruit (see Campari & Tangerine, page 24).

MIXING GLASSES

With a strainer and spoon, they come in 16- and 24-ounce sizes.

MUDDLER

Choose one with a long handle (even a wooden kitchen spoon works well) so you can muddle ingredients right in the cocktail shaker.

STAINLESS STEEL JIGGER (OXO)

This has a two-ounce capacity with both tablespoon and ounce markings on the inside. I love the pour spout and have one designated for both the bar and the kitchen.

TOOTHPICKS

So many cute options out there for olives, ginger, and meatball appetizers (PuTwo makes bamboo cocktail sticks/toothpicks in a peach heart shape).

WINE GLASSES

Wine glasses are designed to enhance the type of wine you are drinking, but (like most things associated with wine) it can seem confusing to match the glasses to the types of wine. If you want to invest in quality glasses, Reidel, Spiegelau, or Zalto are wonderful options. If you have limited storage and budget, one good glass is perfectly fine—go with just a burgundy glass, which can be used for whites, reds, and even Champagne. But if the world is your oyster, there's lots of fantastic glassware that's fun to collect.

Modern glassware often has a bend in the glass that dictates the level to pour to, but otherwise a good rule of thumb is to fill the glass a quarter to a third of the way full, which is about three to four ounces. I like to count to five in my head as I gently pour; this helps me get the right amount without being too geeky.

A fun bit of trivia: A burgundy glass holds 24 ounces and a standard bottle of wine is 25 ounces. Rumor has it that if you poured all of that wine into a crystal burgundy glass, it would break.

Sauvignon blanc: One glass for any type of white wine and rosé. Generally tall and thinner than normal white wine.

Burgundy: If you're only going to invest in one glass, this is your go-to. Can be used for white, red, and Champagne.

Dessert wine: Dessert wine, sherry, port, or Madeira. It's also a good choice for sipping spirits served neat, i.e., tequila or mezcal.

Champagne flute: I love the look of a Champagne coupe, but oftentimes I end up spilling the Champagne all over myself. So these are maybe not as cool looking as a coupe, but they're better at keeping your Champagne in the glass, and they help keep it cool in temperature. A rule of thumb is the drier your Champagne, the bigger the glass should be.

Resources

BAKER CREEK HEIRLOOM SEEDS,
rareseeds.com

COLLEEN HENNESSEY CLAYWORKS,
colleenhennessey.net

FROG HOLLOW FARM (organic fruits and pantry items),
froghollow.com

HERITAGE FOODS (heritage-breed turkey),
heritagefoods.com

KEHOE CARBON COOKWARE,
kehoecarboncookware.com

LA TIENDA (cazuelas and roasted piquillo peppers),
tienda.com

PENNY POUND ICE (beautiful bulk ice),
pennypoundice.com

RANCHO GORDO (heirloom beans and dried chiles),
ranchogordo.com

THE RARE WINE COMPANY (wine, Madeira, and olive
oil), rarewineco.com

THE SOURCE IMPORTS (wine),
thesourceimports.com

WOODLAND HILLS WINE COMPANY,
whwc.com

IN THE SANTA BARBARA AREA

BOTANIK (home goods, tableware, décor),
2329 Lillie Ave., Summerland, CA 93067

COAST 2 COAST COLLECTION (tableware, home décor),
1114 State St., Ste. 10, Santa Barbara, CA 93101

CENTER FOR URBAN AGRICULTURE AT FAIRVIEW
GARDENS (nonprofit organic farm, produce stand, and
educational center), 598 N. Fairview Ave., Goleta, CA
93117

EUROPEAN DELI MARKET (dried herbs, feta, spices),
4422 Hollister Ave., Santa Barbara, CA 93110

FIELD + FORT (home and garden living),
2580 Lillie Ave., Summerland, CA 93067

HUDSON GRACE (tableware, home goods), Montecito
Country Mart, 1014 Coast Village Rd., Ste. F, Santa
Barbara, CA 93108

ISLAND SEED AND FEED (organic starts and feed),
29 S. Fairview Ave., Goleta, CA 93117

LA BELLA ROSA (prepared masa for tamales),
1411 San Andres St., Santa Barbara, CA 93101

THE LIQUOR & WINE GROTTO,
1271 Coast Village Rd., Montecito, CA 93108

PIEDRASASSI (wine, bread, Dijon mustard,
and the best red wine vinegar), piedrasassi.com

PIERRE LAFOND (tableware, home goods),
516 San Ysidro Rd., Montecito, CA 93108

SANTA BARBARA CERTIFIED FARMERS MARKET
(Saturdays), 119 E. Cota St., Santa Barbara, CA 93101

SEA STEPHANIE FISH (Santa Barbara sea urchin
and other fresh, sustainable seafood),
seastephaniefish.com

TAQUERIA EL BAJIO (fresh tortillas to go, and
chorizo and eggs while you're at it),
129 N. Milpas St., Santa Barbara, CA 93103

TINO'S ITALIAN GROCERY (porcini cubes, superfino
Carnaroli rice, pancetta),
210 W. Carrillo St., Santa Barbara, CA 93101

Acknowledgments

It's been my honor to work with an amazingly accomplished team of unparalleled talent, artistry, and tenacity. Thank you, Gemma and Andy Ingalls, Jeanne Kelley, Sarah Tenaglia, Rita Sowins, Julie Robles, Rajat Parr, Suzanne Goin, and Maiya Roddick-Fuller. Every single one of you collaborated in a way that made this project more beautiful, more meaningful, and more fun than I could have ever imagined.

Colleen Dunn Bates, working with you and your team at Prospect Park Books has been a joy. Thank you for your ingenious editorial talent and for taking a chance on a home cook with a dream.

There are countless people who have influenced me—in the kitchen, in the bar, and in the garden. Chris Robles, who guided me in culinary and wine pursuits and coached me through preparing food for intimidating wine dinners. We miss you every day. Ricarda Gonzalez, Irma Aguirre, and Gabriella Gomez, three strong and beautiful women who taught me everything I know about cooking in the Mexican kitchen. Julie Robles, my dear friend, talented chef, and sounding board. Kim Schiffer, whose passion for beautiful ingredients is as awe-inspiring as it is contagious. Juventino Gonzalez, who made me wonderful iron tools that I didn't even know I needed. My garden mentor for more than fifteen years, Pat Omweg, who is a wealth of inspiration and cultivation.

Kyle Irwin, thank you for your spectacular wit, talent, and generosity. Donald Link, Benedetta Vitali, Cal Stamenov, and Robbie Wilson, thank you for years of culinary mentorship, and…Robbie, thanks for Lawson's egg salad sandwiches. Mollie Ahlstrand, thank you for so many special family meals and influential trips to Rome with the girls. Shiji Nohara, thank you for the inspiring treks through the culinary world and beautiful bars of Tokyo. Jill Cohen, thank you for introducing me to a wonderfully talented team. Thank you, Marcella Caputo and Reny Salamon, the best makeup and hair team. Amy Mogis, Molly Hutto, and Ernesto Juarez, thank you for helping make things so beautiful.

I am humbled by the wonderful people who have supported and encouraged me to write this book throughout the years. Thank you for your constant support, insight, collaboration, and charming ways: Leah Watson (you are the pole to my tetherball), Kim Yorio, Katie Scheffey, Dewey and Stephanie Nicks, Joanna Kerns, Les Firestein, David Crane, and Jeffrey Klarik. Thank you to my sisters, Patricia and Desiree for always believing in me. And to all of our friends and family who gather around our kitchen island on a regular basis, I adore you.

Index

About the Author

VALERIE RICE was born and raised in Southern California, and the California lifestyle is apparent in all her endeavors. A serial entertainer, master gardener, passionate margarita maker, and skilled home cook, Valerie shares her passions on her popular food and lifestyle site, eatdrinkgarden.com, as well as on her EatDrinkGarden Instagram account. Valerie has been featured in *Sunset, House Beautiful, Santa Barbara Magazine*, and *Flutter* and has appeared on *Access Hollywood Live* and Hallmark's *Home & Family*. She lives in Santa Barbara with her husband, two daughters, a couple of labradoodles, and a coop full of chickens.

Published by Prospect Park Books
2359 Lincoln Avenue
Altadena, California 91001
www.prospectparkbooks.com

Distributed by Consortium Books Sales & Distribution
www.cbsd.com

Library of Congress Cataloging-in-Publication Data
Names: Rice, Valerie, author. | Ingalls, Andrew, photographer. | Ingalls, Gemma, photographer.
Title: Lush life : food & drinks from the garden
Identifiers: LCCN 2020039644 (print) | LCCN 2020039645 (ebook) | ISBN 9781945551970 (hardcover) | ISBN 9781945551987 (epub)
Subjects: LCSH: Cooking, American--California style. | Gardening. | Beverages. | Seasonal cooking. | LCGFT: Cookbooks.
Classification: LCC TX715.2.C34 R53 2021 (print) | LCC TX715.2.C34 (ebook) | DDC 641.5/64--dc23
LC record available at https://lccn.loc.gov/2020039644
LC ebook record available at https://lccn.loc.gov/2020039645

Photography by Gemma & Andrew Ingalls; photo styling by Jeanne Kelley & Valerie Rice
Author photo by Dewey Nicks
Designed by Rita Sowins / Sowins Design
Recipe editing by Sarah Tenaglia

First edition, first printing
Printed in China